HOW TO
BE A
FOOTBALL
MANAGER

HOW TO BE A FOOTBALL MANAGER

IAN HOLLOWAY

H
HEADLINE

First published in 2022 by
HEADLINE PUBLISHING GROUP

1

Cataloguing in Publication Data is available from the British Library

Hardback ISBN: 978 1 4722 9859 1

Designed and typeset by EM&EN
Printed and bound in Great Britain by Clays Ltd, Elcograf S.p.A.

Headline's policy is to use papers that are natural, renewable and recyclable
products and made from wood grown in well-managed forests and other
controlled sources. The logging and manufacturing processes are expected
to conform to the environmental regulations of the country of origin.

HEADLINE PUBLISHING GROUP
An Hachette UK Company
Carmelite House
50 Victoria Embankment
London EC4Y 0DZ

www.headline.co.uk
www.hachette.co.uk

For my wonderful wife, Kim

Contents

Foreword by Tony Pulis xi

Introduction: Welcome to My World xv

1. The Three Es – My Principles of Play 1

2. Building Your Empire 13

3. What's In Your Toolbox? 23

4. Pre-season 31

5. 'Off-piste' Coaching 47

6. Player Acquisitions 63

7. Picking Your Starting XI – and dealing with the fallout 76

8. Fielding a Weakened Team (even when it isn't) 82

9. Management Myths: Part 1 87

10. Centre-forwards: Handle with Care 106

11. The Post-Match Glass of Wine 115

12. Contract Negotiations 126

13. Press Conferences and the Media 138

14. Referees: How (and how not) to Deal With Them 151

15. Working the Chairman 169

16. Anger Management 185

17. Dealing with Supporters. My Way 191

18. Management Myths: Part 2 198

19. Football in a Pandemic 210

20. The Managerial Merry-Go-Round 224

21. Gardening Leave 238

22. Taking Inspiration From Wherever You Can Find It 243

23. Believe It or Not! 248

24. The Crème de la Crème 280

Acknowledgements 289

Index 292

'Yeah, I'm all of that plus a bag of chips.'

FOREWORD

by Tony Pulis

I first came across Ian Holloway almost fifty years ago at Bristol Rovers when he was just a young schoolboy.

Rovers were renowned for bringing young players through, in particular from South Wales and Bristol, and with the senior mentors that the club possessed, it was no surprise there was so much youthful talent that progressed through to league football.

Rovers were a community club and there was a wonderful feeling of togetherness. Young players were made aware of the standards they needed to aim for and the rules they needed to abide by, and there was a fantastic level of common sense that each and every player bought into.

Ian was a talented lad both on and off the pitch – his paintings and sketches were amazing, and nobody else I know has ever knocked down as many interior walls in as many homes and then nonchalantly put them back together again! Blessed with enormous energy levels, even with all the above going on, nobody could run or would run further than Ian on a Saturday afternoon: his fitness levels and nervous energy levels were off the charts.

It didn't take him long to establish himself in the Rovers first team playing wide on the right, and after a period of consistently good performances, he caught the eye of Dave Bassett (also known as 'Harry'), who signed him for Wimbledon. Ian joined a club who were on a very steep upward curve. That season Wimbledon won promotion to top-flight football and although Ian played nearly half the season, I could tell by our discussions that he found it very difficult to settle into the rhythms of the team and to bond with the individuals he shared a dressing room with. At the time it affected his confidence and after less than a year at Wimbledon, followed by two short spells at Brentford and Torquay, he was on his way back to Bristol Rovers.

Gerry Francis was Rovers' manager at the time, and he actually bought Ian back with his own money! But the real stroke of genius was switching Ian to a central midfield role. Gerry was the catalyst in propelling Ian's career to a level he had always aspired to. His energy and ability to win the ball and then play it simply to more creative individuals proved to be the making of him during a very productive playing time at Rovers and then at QPR, where I would say Ian, in my eyes, played his best football of a career that spanned more than 600 games.

Foreword

My introduction to management was this quote from a very experienced football man who I'll not name here – he told me, 'Management is about being in the shit – you're either ankle deep, knee deep or up to your neck in it, but one thing's for sure, you're always in it.'

It came as no surprise to me when Rovers came calling again for Ian, this time to take up a player-manager role. There was no way Ian would turn down a chance to go back to his spiritual home.

Ian would go on to manage eight different clubs, winning promotion with QPR, Blackpool and Crystal Palace. Blackpool was the standout achievement in my opinion, not only through winning the play-offs and gaining promotion, but by the way they took the Premier League by storm, which also led to tremendous praise from people inside and outside the game.

Although Ian has gained a reputation for his witty answers and off-the-wall summarisations of different topics, nobody manages that many clubs or games without having knowledge, passion and determination, and he has all of that in abundance.

I have already expressed the tremendous respect I had for my own upbringing at Bristol Rovers and the mentors who shaped our lives. During my time at Rovers, I married my wife Debbie and when our first child was born, I asked a young Ian Holloway to be our son Anthony's godfather. I had got to know Ian's mum and dad and felt he would be a great example to Anthony as he was growing up.

Ian's dad, Bill, was a wonderful man who idolised his son, and Jean was a mother full of love, protection and comfort – wonderful traits to take on yourself when the time calls. That call came eventually when Ian met Kim, and both struck up a loving relationship that led to them getting married.

Early on in the relationship, Kim was diagnosed with a serious illness. Ian's response and reaction was full of love, care and protection. He idolises Kim, and to this day he will always put her first, second and third.

During their marriage, the couple brought into the world four wonderful children but with a compilation of different challenges which neither Ian nor Kim had ever confronted before. It would and could have been really difficult for any normal human being, and especially with Ian's 'day job', but like always, he and Kim picked the baton up and sprinted into the unknown with gusto and patience that remain such an inspiration to me.

All four of Ian and Kim's children must be so proud of how they persevered and conquered such a difficult period.

Yes, love, care and protection run through the veins of the Holloways, and for all that Ian has achieved, my gold medal goes to him for the way he has looked after what nobody else sees – his wonderful family.

Tony Pulis, Dorset, July 2022

INTRODUCTION

Welcome to My World . . .

Who'd be a football manager?

It's an emotional rollercoaster that when you're riding it, you can't wait to get off, but once the ride stops, you want to get straight back on again and feel that adrenaline rush.

If you love the game as much as I do – and you don't have to have played at any level or managed, either – you'll understand exactly what I'm talking about.

I'm the lucky one because I've been able to be on the pitch creating some magical moments, or in the dugout making decisions that can change the outcomes of major matches. I've always known it's a privilege to be able to do what I did for forty years as a player and a manager, and in the pages that follow, I'm going to try and explain what being a football manager is really all about.

I'll share some of the funniest and saddest stories asso-ciated with my management career along the way, but this isn't a book purely about anecdotes, arguments, laughter and tears. It's about how to be a football manager, what to expect, what you should and shouldn't do and everything in-between.

Being a manager is an emotional juggernaut on which you find out about your weaknesses, your barriers and then there's your ego . . . oh my God, it's horrendous! But it has also been a genuine privilege, as well as a chaotic madhouse and a breathless journey from start to finish.

Have I done things the way other managers have done? Probably not. I'm different, I know that, and have always followed my own path, but as a manager you never stop learning – and that was as true in my first job at Bristol Rovers as it was in the last one I had at Grimsby Town.

This is a book that details every aspect of being a football manager, and there have been many moments of elation, anger, joy, frustration and satisfaction in my twenty years on the touchline – as you are about to discover. I'll take you inside the dressing room, into the boardroom, onto the training pitch, away on pre-season and into matches, and I'll try and dispel as many management myths as I can along the way – not to mention my tips and tricks to survive and thrive in management. And should you ever find yourself in a dressing room with a load of horses, we've got that covered, too!

Saying it like it is, that's me in a nutshell. I'm not proud of it all, and it can sometimes come back and bite you on the ass. But my whole life as a manager was based on letting people know where they stood with me. I think it's absolutely vital you do that and tell them what's expected of them. I'll fight for them if it's needed, and I feel I've had that reciprocated from most of the people I've worked with.

I know it hasn't always gone well but, wherever I've been, I genuinely wanted it to, and I genuinely tried my best. At the end of the day, isn't that what life is all about? Being the best version of yourself you can be?

So, fasten your seatbelts, put on your crash helmets, and prepare to enter my crazy world and by the end of this book, you might want to give it a go yourself – or be put off for life!

Ian Holloway, Wiltshire, July 2022

1

The Three Es – My Principles of Play

As a manager, the bottom line for me is:
'This is how I play, this is what I want and if you
don't do it, you won't be here.'

When you are a football manager, the first thing you've got to decide is how you want your players to follow you, what you want them to be and who you want them to be – so you have to make some pretty big decisions from the word go.

You have to decide how you are going to lead your troops, so I try to simplify all that and I'd suggest anyone who wants to be a manager does the same, because it is vitally important.

The words I've chosen all begin with the same letter, and I call them the Three Es. This is something I always start with and ask the players to bring with them, every morning, no matter what the score was in the last game and whether we were in a good or bad run or whatever – I wanted them to play for me, with the Three Es in mind.

I'd write it on a flipchart or a chalkboard then tell them that the first thing I want to see straight away is **Encouragement** – of yourself and others. Encouragement of yourself – because some of us criticise ourselves, drop our shoulders and our body language says all you need to know about how we are feeling. If you do that, you're not instantly in the game and you start moaning at everybody else. Encouragement of others – because that's what I demand from my lads: willing your teammates on and supporting them when they need it most, and that's a basic requirement.

So, I demand encouragement at all times, no matter what the situation. Once you've got that mindset, you have a positive attitude, and you can start spreading that to everyone else. It's infectious. Quite simple, isn't it?

The next 'E' is for **Enthusiasm**. If I'm your manager I want you to bring that in abundance and I want yours to match mine every morning, so if you see me down, you can be down too, but if you don't see me like that, I want you to match my enthusiasm at the very least. I told all my players they'd never beat my enthusiasm, because that's who I am and I've got it in bucketloads, but I wanted to see it in them as well.

The third 'E' requirement is **Enjoyment** – I want to see you enjoying the way we're playing, the way we're training and going about things. I don't want to see anyone ever down, so without the first two – encouragement and enthusiasm –

you'll never get the last one, anyway, so work on the first two, and I'm sure we'll get the last one.

That's what I'm looking for, every single day, and that will either get you in the team, when you're displaying those qualities, or out of the team, if I don't see those words being absorbed and taken into your daily life.

Explaining the Three Es – my three principles of play – is something I locked down at the very first team meeting I had at every single club I ever managed.

I found that nine times out of ten I would be joining a club that's in trouble – there was only one occasion in my career that I started at a club that was in a fantastic position and that was Crystal Palace, but that's very unusual and an exception to the rule. I carried the Three Es with me because I wanted to see those behaviours, attributes, attitudes – call them what you like – in my players. That's what I believe got me to be a manager in the first place, because I played with those Three Es.

If anyone didn't show me what I was looking for and then came to see me to ask why they weren't playing, I could say, 'Hang on a minute, are you playing with my Three Es?' No, you're not, so what's wrong with you?' – and sometimes that brought out other things that they were having trouble with along the lines of, 'Well, I can't be enthusiastic or encourage others because blah, blah, blah' so it actually sets some parameters for them and allows them to get stuff off their chest.

Map out your principles of play from minute one. That is my suggestion for any new manager. Then the players know what you're about and where the boundaries lie. This is the ground you'll be stood on – it won't be thin ice – but if I can see those three basic requirements, you'll have a good chance of being alright with me.

Ollie's Tip: You have to explain how you want the team to play, but at a new club you have to assess what you've got first and what best suits those players. You can't just come in with a style you want them to play – unless you think you can change them all, which is nigh on impossible.

So, if you think you can be a manager, what would you do? What would your words be to inspire people? It really does help to know what it is you are demanding and be able to put it across clearly and in a simple way.

The other thing that really does help – and I don't live by it myself, because I have a character default and an anger issue (but more on that later) – is remembering that:

$$E + R = O$$

Don't worry, I'm not going to go all Albert Einstein on you – it simply means: an Event in your life, plus your Response to that event, equals the Outcome.

In football we can't control what happens on the pitch and anyone who thinks differently needs their feckin' head sorting – the ref might make a decision we don't agree with, a teammate might make a mistake or get sent off, whatever – but we must have a positive response at all times to the event that's occurred. This is a key principle when you're playing for me. Whatever the event is, even if it's a bad one, please come and tell me about it. I'll take the pressure off you, but I want a positive response to it, because otherwise you're going to get two negatives and two negatives can never make a positive. Simple maths again, right? And a simple and straightforward way of saying: THIS IS WHAT I WANT FROM YOU.

And it's not just football. In your general life, how many events are you in control of? You can try to be in control, but that's what makes me laugh about football – 'we controlled the second half, we were in control of the game' – you're never in control of the goddamned game! You never are and you never will be because that ball can go anywhere and you can try and do this or that with it, but the other team will be doing their best to try and stop you. As a plumber, you're in control of the job once you've got it – there's nobody pulling the pipes off the wall as you're putting them on; there's nobody taking the boiler out after you've just installed it and there aren't thousands of people demanding you do it a hundred different ways.

When I played in midfield, I'd try and dominate the midfield area, but somebody else would try and stop me, and I had to try and beat him – and some days, I couldn't, but the truth is I never ever gave up on anything because of my mindset, so it really does help you. For an event in your life that you're not in control of, try and work out your response and try and make it a positive one.

QPR were having a terrible time of it in 2001 and going through administration, so as manager I decided to get an American motivator over called Jack Canfield – I'd read some of his stuff in a book and he had representatives going out to spread his philosophy, so I think it cost us about £3,000 to have them come over to talk to my team. Their mantra was that it didn't matter what happens around you, if you have a positive mindset, you can achieve anything. There were three of them and they came in for three days, sat us down and it helped my senior players, some of the mid-aged group and certainly helped me react to things more positively because everything was crashing down around me.

They showed a video of two guys who were sat down with headphones on. One of them was being told that everything he was doing was useless and he was getting everything so wrong, he was this, that and the other and then they asked him at the end to put his arms up while they did a strength test to see how hard he could push, and he was as weak as a kitten! The other guy was being told he was brilliant and everything he did was fantastic and that everything good they were doing was because of him, and at the end, they did the same strength test and he pushed so hard you wouldn't believe it. Their point was that your mindset can be changed with positive talk, which back then I didn't know was even possible.

They related that video to all the external criticism the club was receiving, and told the lads they were still playing for this famous club and that it was a privilege to be playing for that shirt and they bigged us right up. It was brilliant.

Then they made you tell something about your life that the group didn't know about – it could be anything – before you were asked to choose a song about your life that you thought summed you up as a person.

One of the lads told us about how he'd lost his mum as a kid and none of us had known about it – he had tears rolling down his cheeks as he spoke about it, and he hadn't realised he'd had a problem that he'd never fully dealt with.

When it came to me, I told them I had this thing about my nose and that I'd been terrified I'd never get a girlfriend because my nose was so massive. I had a big hang-up about my hooter, but I felt much better when I opened up about it to the group. The song that I chose was Chumbawamba's

'Tubthumping' – the lyrics 'I get knocked down, but I get up again' summed me up as a person.

It was actually an incredible insight into what the mind is capable of. Everything at QPR had been all wrong, it was all broken, but I was like, 'Nah, it's alright, we're going to come out of this like a phoenix, but while we're in it, I need some positivity'. And we ended up getting promoted that season in spite of everything.

It got me wondering about Jack Canfield, too. What if his name had been Jack Can'tfield? He'd have had to change professions!

Why am I sharing all of this? It's because you're not just a manager, you're a motivator and the players follow you – and if you're down, they follow you again. There are so many things that can get you down in football. For example, you have a one in three chance of losing every time you go out there. So, if you don't win – and there's a sixty-six per cent chance you won't – you've failed. If you win, happy days, brilliant, that's what everyone wants, tick the box, away you go. If you draw, you've dropped two points and if you lose, you've dropped three and you've failed – and there's no way of hiding it. If Man City or Liverpool draw three in a row, oh my God, that is terrible – a crisis, even. If Norwich draw three in a row, everyone says how well they are doing. You have to make the 'fail' a positive, each and every time. That's very difficult to do when it involves a team, because it's easy for a group of people to wander off and blame someone else and not themselves, and if you get that in any dressing room, you are never going to be a good manager because you haven't dealt with it properly.

> ***Ollie's Tip:*** *It's really important you have things written down at home or etched in your mind to occasionally check 'where am I?' because it's very easy to forget what your principles are. As a manager, if you have those principles and you don't follow them, even just once, you're dead. You do not cross your own lines, ever, because people won't follow you. Ask Boris Johnson.*

Not everyone is cut out for management and some people are comfortable just following and we need them just as much. But I know what a good leader is – I'm not saying I'm one, though I know what their habits are.

Managers have to deal with themselves first and understand who they are before they can help anyone else. Whenever I do anything, I'm my own biggest critic because I never feel that it's good enough. But when I talk to my players, I talk to them as though I'm their conscience and say that they should be talking to themselves in a similar way – and when they listen, they can do things so much better than they actually thought they could.

That was part of the joy of management for me because I'd had such a struggle myself – with myself – that I found it easier to talk to players and help them come out of their shells and help them believe in themselves more. That's also about relaxing them as well, because I don't know anyone who has done something really well when they're tense and feeling under pressure.

> *Food for thought: I wish I was more like I am as a manager in most aspects of my everyday life, because the other side of me comes out then – and we've all got different sides, haven't we? The side of my personality that finds things funny has really helped me at times, but I also think my sense of humour has hindered me as well. If I'd had a Scots accent, for instance, instead of this Bristolian one, would I have been taken a bit more seriously? I think the answer is probably yes.*

Being a manager is also about making everyone and everything feel better and that you're moving forward the whole time, because the minute the lads believe they're stopped still or that another club is improving more than they are, they don't like it. You can have absolute chaos everywhere, so long as you're striving to progress things – they will follow you, then.

Just remember that tactics and principles of play are

intertwined. What do Ian Holloway's QPR do? What do Ian Holloway's Leicester City do? What do Ian Holloway's Crystal Palace do? You should know, as a player, what I want you to do, no matter what tactics I give you.

If I played you at left-back, right-back, centre-back or wherever – you should still know that I'm not changing my basic principles. I'd be like, 'You understand those don't you – but on top of that, I want you to stay a bit wider today. I don't need you coming off that line, can you do that? Great. This player's got a wonderful left foot, I want you to show him in on the right so he's running inside, and he won't feel comfortable, can you do that?' That's tactics. I've got hundreds of them, but what I'm trying to do is get the principles of play to be second nature and you can adjust, tweak, or change tactics as and when you need to in order to try and win a game. You can't control what's going on around you. Look at Steven Gerrard telling the Liverpool players at Norwich 'this does not slip' – then a week later, what happens? He slips and then Chelsea's Demba Ba runs though, scores and Liverpool end up losing the title.

Against Crystal Palace they were 3–0 with ten minutes to go and they end up drawing 3–3, so were they ever in control of those games or their destiny? No. You never are. You might think you are, but you're not. You might 'dominate the ball', but you're never in control and I despise it when I hear that description of a game, because it's lazy and it doesn't mean anything.

As a manager, the bottom line for me is: 'This is how I play, this is what I want and if you don't do it, you won't be here'. I can't stand negative people and I think that's what helped me stay in a job so long because when my teams lose the ball, they don't stand around moaning at each other, they try and win it back before anything else. That's a positive outcome from a response to an event. Remember, E + R = O.

2

Building Your Empire

We haven't all been football managers, but we've all
bought a second-hand car . . .Whether it's a car or
a footballer, you need a full service history.

The most important thing in management is to have good
people around you, and in order to do that you need great
connections and for me, that means getting in place a
scouting network of people who know exactly what you are
looking for in a player. That is something that takes a long
time to build and it needs to be nurtured and cared for,
because these are the people who will be your eyes and ears
at every club you go to.

It's crucial that you bring the right staff into your environment because you're trying to create a place where you can
achieve anything you want. As a manager, if you start your
journey without those cogs in the wheel, you are nowhere
near ready to move forward. It's important to do the work
beforehand, because if you can get seventy-five per cent of

the people you bring in right, you've got a chance of success; but if you don't, you're not going to have a career the way football is today. You need to build your connections from all around the world, of people who love football and go and watch it all the time, and they can sometimes just be good football people with an eye for a player.

You need to express what you're looking for in each position and if you can do that to your chief scout, who basically deals with all those people, you're on the right road. I used to have a guy called Graham Bird work for me and, like me, he was a Bristolian. He was mad on football and went everywhere to watch games even if he wasn't given petrol money. Gary Penrice ('Pen') – who, as you read through this book, you will come to understand is one of my closest and most trusted friends in football – was my chief scout for much of my career, found Graham for me and he turned out to be just the right fella to do what I wanted at that time. I even asked Pen if he could get two or three more like Graham and we'd pay their expenses and maybe a retainer if I liked them. That's how you build your network, brick by brick.

I'd only get to talk with these guys every now and then because I was so busy, but I was well aware of what they were doing and people like that become part of your management structure.

Their job is to spot someone or deliver a report on a player who we've been keeping tabs on, then Pen will do his bit and come to me and say, 'I know what you want me to find, I think I've found it, but you need to go and have a look', because if that player turned up and didn't get on with me, we'd have a big problem.

It's vital you find players that are good people first and foremost, and then you try and make them better people as well as better players. You have to make them realise that this is not just how they are going to play football; they have to understand that I am in every bit of their lives, now. You want to get on board our train and go where we're going? Then you've got to please me. And if you're not looking after your missus, not looking after your kids, if you're not doing that right, I'm not gonna have you.

> *Ollie's Tip: When a new player joins the club, I insist on meeting his wife or girlfriend and ask them, 'How's he doing? How's he treating you? Does he treat you like a princess? If not, why not? Why are you putting up with that?' Because if they're not right together, you've got problems further down the line.*

I ask where they're going to live, what are they going to do, what are their plans – you've got to care, and I think most people don't realise that and when it goes wrong, they wonder why it doesn't work. And if you're limited with how much you can spend, how important is it that you get the right one? I've turned away hundreds of players because Pen spotted a character flaw before we made a move.

Maybe their warm-up wasn't good; maybe they threw their arms up in frustration at a teammate during the game; maybe they didn't react well with the fans outside, before or after. They might have ticked all the boxes in terms of ability and have the attributes we were looking for, but if they didn't fit that strict criteria we set down, then it didn't go any further.

I remember with Jason Puncheon, Kenny Jackett had got him scoring goals for Millwall during a loan spell away from Southampton, but for whatever reason things down at St Mary's just weren't right for him. I told Pen I needed a forward to bring to Blackpool in the January transfer window and he said, 'It's got to be Punch. He'd run through brick walls for you.' I spoke to Kenny, and he said that all Punch needed was to be treated with respect, have an arm around him when needed and that he was as honest as the day was long if things didn't go well. Southampton were two divisions down at the time, but Pen had every faith, so I spoke to Punch, and he was happy to come to us. He just didn't want to be in Southampton anymore. We got the loan deal sorted, I put him in, and Pen was spot-on as always because Punch deserved to be playing Premier League football.

Luke Varney was the same. We played Crewe Alexandra in a pre-season friendly and after the game Dario Gradi said,

'Do you mind if I ask you a question? Why haven't you gone in for Luke Varney?'

Varney was a former Crewe player who was now at Derby County where it hadn't really happened for him. I asked if he was available and he said, 'Oh yeah, he's out of contract soon. He's someone who will fit in with your lot all day long, the way you played today. I've got his number if you want it?'

I asked if I would be able to afford him and he said, 'Ollie, he would love to play football that way.' And we ended up taking him on a season-long loan from Derby County.

Food for thought: There were times at Blackpool when we took players on that had established a reputation for being this or that, but we'd seen past that and accepted it was most likely a case of mud sticking because we'd done our homework on them first. The scouts we employed weren't famous and nobody knew their names, but they were so important and well-connected. They were the glue that held our whole ethos together.

We haven't all been football managers, but we've all bought a second-hand car in our lifetime. Do you really trust where it's come from? You've got to dig into it, do your research, check the garage out and the mileage and make sure what you've been told about it is correct. If you buy a new car, you will lose a load of money as soon as you drive it out of the showroom, but that might also give you the peace of mind and give you the satisfaction that you're getting a good one. Whether it's a car or a footballer, you need a full service history.

Frank Lampard got the Chelsea manager's job and there was no way he could have the connections in place that he needed immediately, but if he goes back in ten years' time, he'll have built up that network of trusted connections around him. I actually think he didn't do that bad considering he was fairly new to management, and he brought some very good young players in that were for the benefit of Chelsea in the long term. But were they ready to do what Frank needed them to do, at the time he was there? Probably not. Hopefully, he'll get the time he needs at Everton, but you're never more than two or three defeats away from big trouble.

When I left QPR for Plymouth, I took all my coaching staff with me – Gary Penrice, Tim Breacker and Des Bulpin – and then took all three with me to Leicester City, but after that, it all disbanded. At Blackpool, I went with the existing coaching staff but there was just three of us on the day staff – myself, Steve Thompson the first-team coach and Phil Horner the physio – plus the part-time kitman, Steve Wales ('Walesy'). We also had Matt Williams who did four jobs, and though his title was media officer, he should have been

Blackpool's CEO – but never was. We were as professional as we could be and as cheap as we could be.

Karl Oyston, the chairman, wanted to know everything he could about everyone's role at the club so he asked what Walesy did when the tumble dryers were turning, because he said, in so many words, he wasn't going to pay for him to sit on his backside while he waited for them to finish. He wanted to get the most he could out of everyone, and you worked a full day and then some under his reign. Walesy had to double up as a cabbie in-between to make ends meet, despite doing a full-time kitman's job. I tried to get Walesy an industrial-sized washing machine to use, but Karl thought it was a waste of money, so he had to use three normal washing machines. That's just how Karl was.

I must admit, I would have taken my coach, physio and kitman wherever I went in my management career if I could have done, but they were from good, solid Northern stock and they loved where they were from. At the time of writing, Phil is still at Blackpool and Thommo is at Preston North End. And Matt Williams was incredible, doing four jobs and being a massive help to me during my time there. He was a fantastic scout and we leaned on each other as and when needed and usually after dealing with Karl who was never less than straight as a die. I respected them all as people and because of the values they had – they knew you didn't get anything out of life without hard work and I just admired that. Whatever they did, they made the best out of it; if they were given a box of lemons, they would be the type to say, 'OK. We'll make lemonade.'

When I went to Palace, they were on a different level. The club had an infrastructure that was amazing, and the difference was quite unbelievable. It's incredible what you can achieve when people are motivated about the right things. The infrastructure is so important to keep the club moving forward and, in my experience, you need a two-tier approach. Firstly, have a good academy producing young players who can come through and play for the first team, because there's nothing better than homegrown talent and fans absolutely love it. Secondly, you need a solid scouting network, which takes years and years to build, and that can be made up of anyone and everyone, so long as they love football, have an eye for a player and can then write up a report about them. You keep those scouts on a retainer, pay them petrol money and build them into your knowledge and trust network.

Ollie's Tip: Your scouts are the unsung heroes who keep you in a job, because they are constantly looking for and finding little gems for you.

Palace were a big club who were trying to get back to where they had been and looking to build something special.

Chairman Steve Parish always use to say, 'Why can't we be a top ten Premier League side?' He understood the infrastructure needed to do that and – Leicester apart – when I went to be Palace manager, I had more staff working for me than I'd had at all my other clubs combined. If you look at Palace and Leicester today, I can understand why they are mainstays of the Premier League. You need people out there, watching, analysing and figuring out all the time to give you the best chance of success. The more information you can get from research that your team does, the better manager you are going to be.

It makes me laugh. Sam Allardyce gets labelled as a long-ball merchant or a dinosaur by certain sections of the media, but the truth is he was way ahead of his time with the analysts he put in place at Bolton and the sport scientists, dieticians and goodness knows what else. Big Sam was a pioneer in many ways with the data he received and how he utilised it – because although any club could get the information and stats on opposition players, it's what you do with that data that matters, and he took Bolton Wanderers into Europe and to the brink of Champions League football. That's a manager who gets the most from the staff around him.

Looking back, I likened Blackpool to a corner shop. We had the basics people needed, people liked to pop in and we were a family-run business, but we couldn't do any more than we were doing because the big supermarkets were going to swallow us up. Supermarkets can make their own produce, have their own brands, and sell it cheaper, so they eventually eat up all the corner shops. Palace and Leicester wanted to be supermarkets, if you like, and that was the big difference.

3

What's In Your Toolbox?

'Oh my God . . . how bad is that?'

Getting your house in order to get the best out of your players is essential. You need the tools to do the job, and sometimes you have to be a crafty bastard because that's part of management, too.

At Plymouth, the gym was a Portakabin and I said to the chairman, 'The Portakabin's fine – we've just got to get better equipment in there. If you can buy a bigger Portakabin, good, or put another one next to the one we've got, great, but it's the quality of equipment that I want you to improve and invest in. It doesn't have to be brand new, but it's got to be better than what we've got.'

We managed to find a gym that was upgrading its stuff, so we were able to get what we needed a lot cheaper and as a result, the chairman was happy, though not entirely convinced we would reap the benefits. I said, 'Let's get it installed and I'll go and show the lads' and it made such a difference. I started to teach the players proper weightlifting to improve their muscle mass so they could move quicker and faster and they were keen to buy into all that. Football had stood still for too long and the scientific element of the game was just starting to evolve.

It's about having the right equipment, the right training pitches, the right diet, the right food, and lots of different things. At Blackpool, our training ground was dilapidated and the pitch was awful, so I took our chairman Karl Oyston down to have a look near the start of pre-season. He was adamant from the start.

'We own it so we're not moving.'

Ironically, he'd gone over on his ankle playing British Bulldog with his kids the day before and he was on crutches.

'Fine,' I said, 'but we're supposed to be training on it later this week and I wouldn't run a racehorse on it.' I told him to put his crutches down and walk across the pitch with me – busted ankle or not. And he did.

Seconds later, the penny dropped. 'Oh my God,' he said, 'how bad is that?'

I told him that it wasn't good enough. I wanted a team that could make slick passing moves, but there was no way we could do that on the training ground with that surface. 'We've been down the road to another training facility, had a look around and it's good enough for the time being,' I told him. 'We've done a deal, you go there and do a better deal and we'll come back here when it's all been sorted, but right now that's not ready and we can't train on that.'

I told the lads it wouldn't be forever – it was about 10–12 weeks in total – and that the owner was going to spend some money on the training ground. I made him do it and they were happy with me because they didn't think I'd be able to convince him. But I did!

> ***Ollie's Tip:*** *For me, striving to get better and improve is what life is all about, but you have to start from within first and that was what I did as a manager – I made sure that I could manage myself and lead myself before I could lead anyone else. That's how it starts.*

How to manage room service

I didn't normally get told off during my time as Blackpool manager, but there was one occasion I got called into Karl Oyston's office where he asked me, 'What's going on? Have you been keeping your eye on these players?' I asked him what he meant, and he said, 'Well, we're feeding them and then they're ordering room service afterwards.'

'Nah,' I said, 'my lads wouldn't do that.'

'Well, who's ordering this food then? Look at these hotel bills?'

I had a look and there were chips and beer on an invoice charged to the club. I told Karl that wasn't right, but he said, 'I'm telling you, keep your eye out for it. I'm not paying for this again after we've just fed them half-an-hour before. They should bloody well pay for it themselves and you should know what they're eating.'

I didn't say anything to the lads, but on our next away trip, I asked them at the evening meal if they were all OK, had eaten enough or needed anything else. When they went back to their rooms, I went to the receptionist and told her that if any of my players ordered room service, she was to come over and tell me because myself and the backroom staff always ate slightly later.

I had ordered my starter, but it hadn't arrived yet when the receptionist came over and said that one of the lads had ordered some chips and two pints of lager for their room. She said she had told them no, but I told her to call them back and say it was fine – but when the food and drink was ready, she was to let me know so I could go up with the member of staff and then I would deliver it personally.

It turned out to be the room of Brett Ormerod and Keith Southern – two of my senior players and I was thinking, 'Hang about. What's going on here? They know the rules.' So, when the young lad knocked on their room, I knew they'd look through the little spyglass in the door first, so I waited until they did and then quickly took the tray as I heard the door being unlocked and stood there with the two pints and bowl of chips. Brett opens the door, sees me and his jaw drops.

'Oh shit, gaffer!'

'Yes, move out the way and I'll bring your room service in!'

I put the tray down on the table. 'What are you pair of nuggets doing?' I said.

They didn't know what to say so I said, 'Tell me, if you were at home on a Friday evening, what would you do?'

'Gaffer, it's OK,' Brett said, 'I always have a drink and it's fine.'

'And you eat chips?'

'Yeah.'

I looked at Keith. 'Well, what about you?'

'No, I don't usually,' he said, 'but on the last few away games I have, because I'm with him.'

I told them OK, they could keep doing it and that this order was on me, but going forward, they had to pay their own bills for any room service because the chairman had found out. I don't recall any extras appearing on our hotel bills after that.

The moral of this story? Sometimes you need to be a bit flexible with your thinking and being open and honest is better than telling a player or players not to do something because they will go ahead and do it anyway more times than not. You can't teach an old dog new tricks but give it the odd biscuit as a treat every now and then and they behave better. If not, they'll soon be out the door.

> ***Food for thought:*** *Having to tell players you don't want them and you're letting them go is one of the hardest parts of management. The broken dreams and financial burden for them and their families is awful and it's something I found really hard.*

At QPR, when we went into administration, I had to let all our young players go and some of them had four years left on their contracts, but the club were only able to pay them fifteen per cent of what they were owed because we couldn't pay their wages anymore. So they had to accept a small fraction of what we'd originally agreed with them in order to be able to go somewhere else on a free transfer.

There were about ten or eleven young players who I had to say the same thing to, and their mums and dads were in tears and some of the kids were as well, but I had to explain that if they didn't go, the club might go under. It was the hardest part of the job and I hated it because I loved to inspire and make people believe they could be better than they ever thought they could, so the opposite of that is to tell them you don't want them anymore and they're not part of your plans.

Going into administration, I was left with seven players, no goalkeeper, two long-term injuries and had hardly any staff left because the administrators had got rid of them and it was all about who I brought in for little or no money, but I never made it an excuse.

I always found honesty was the best policy, so I'd sit them down, tell them they weren't in my plans and explain to them why that was, wish them good luck and promise I'd give them a good recommendation if they needed me to. Having said all that, it's a really tough thing to do and you can't get past the fact that it's a form of rejection.

One of the worst experiences was in my last job at Grimsby where I had eleven players out of contract and we didn't know when football was going to start again (this was during the first COVID lockdown), so we couldn't offer them new deals. Out of those eleven, I wanted to re-sign five of them, but I wasn't given the opportunity to do that because we didn't know when we'd be playing again, and the chairman didn't want to pay players that wouldn't be playing as he still needed to honour the ones who were still under contract 100 per cent, like he was.

'Ollie,' he said, 'how can I sign players when we haven't got the go-ahead yet? That's coming out of my bank. We'll have to sign them when we get the go-ahead.'

It was an impossible situation and we ended up losing them all.

Life is about knowing where you stand, even if it's the worst place you can be, and you never forget that person that tells you the truth. I had it with Dave Bassett at Wimbledon who on the day I signed said, 'I'm not sure I want you. I think I've got someone who's better than you.'

I said, 'Oh right, who's that?'

He said, 'Dennis Wise – he's out on loan in Sweden. But my assistant likes you – I've seen you once, but he's seen you fourteen times and I'm going with his judgement. What have you got to say about that?'

So, I said, 'OK, I'll show you.' But he was probably right about Wisey! I actually thought the way he did it was fantastic, and I never forgot it. He called himself Harry the Absolute Bastard. He was right in your face, and it was like, wow! What he was looking for was a character reaction and I thought I gave it, but he thought I was weak and I ended up leaving and going to Brentford, but I admired the directness and honesty that Harry demonstrated and I brought that into my management. Definitely one for the toolbox! Not all managers do that – some are very different, and you need to find your own way. As a manager, you need to tell them what they *need* to hear, not what they *want* to hear.

4

Pre-season

'Running from A to B? Fine. Figuring out coordinates to find a route with my lot? What could possibly go wrong?'

Electronic tags, air and sea rescue helicopters searching for my players and suspected fugitives on the run? Welcome to pre-season, Ian Holloway style!

Pre-season is your bedrock as a football manager. It is where you lay the foundations on which you are going to build – and that's the best way I can describe it. You want your pre-season to be really good and productive, because the players are away from their families, wives and girl-friends and you've got them twenty-four hours a day so you can influence them, see what they're doing and what they are about, while all the time they are building camaraderie among the group which is a crucial ingredient for any team.

It's about increasing fitness levels and suffering together and understanding what your team is about. I wanted it to be a bit like the SAS training – a test of character – and I always tried to find trained professionals from outside football to help us.

I like to have the players for at least ten days, so I can get three sessions in a day into them without them breaking down. That's thirty sessions in total of high-intensity drills; after they've had six or seven weeks off, it is absolutely crucial to push them to their limits.

The last thing I want is matches at this stage and when you do start playing, you want the easiest games first then build up gradually to the hardest match at the end. But there's never really any such thing as a friendly because amateurs want to beat you, and once you face another professional side both teams just want to win and inevitably it ends up in some kind of brawl that can often end with someone getting injured. That's the last thing you need at this time.

Ollie's Tip: For a professional footballer, if you don't get five to six weeks' full training into you before the new campaign kicks off, I believe you're on your way to having a bad season as an individual.

I always knew exactly the sort of work I wanted for my players physically, because in reality, you're trying to break them and then put them back together. I found the RAF helped me enormously. They have bases all around the country and when I wasn't at a big club, or we didn't have much money, we went to the RAF base in Aylesbury one year and RAF Kinloss in Scotland another year – though after Kinloss, I chose slightly more professional places like hotel facilities with wonderful complexes to try and up the ante every time.

Let's begin with RAF Kinloss, which was a bit different because at QPR I had issues going on with one of my players who came to me on the first day of pre-season and said that he was in terrible trouble and was up on a sexual assault charge that he vehemently denied. I made him look me in the eye and asked if he did it and I believed him when he said, 'No gaffer, I didn't and would never do anything like that. But the police are charging me and putting an ankle bracelet on me, so I won't be able to go away.'

'Well, that's not happening, son,' I said to him. 'If you want to play for me, you have to come away with us – who do I need to speak to?'

'I don't know what you mean. I've been told by the cops that I can't go away.'

I told him that I'd have to ask if I could take stewardship of him and make sure he needed to be wherever he needed to be at the right time, observe any curfews and do whatever the authorities required, because he had to come with us on pre-season; otherwise, I wouldn't be using him. And he was a good player, too.

I went to the local police, had a chat and they said it was fine for him to travel, so long as he was under curfew and I was in control of his movements at all times. I had to sign papers confirming that I would ensure all the conditions were met, and arrangements to check-in with the local police in Kinloss were made.

We flew up to Scotland in early July and the RAF instructors were soon doing their fitness drills with the squad and all seemed to be going well. I had to take my player to the local police station at 5 p.m. each day to sign in and the first few days went swimmingly . . . that is, until orienteering day.

Normally, in my plan, day four would have been cross-country day, but the instructors told me they wanted to test the lads and do something different. They wanted to take them orienteering, but I said they'd never done it before and some of them were not the brightest, so just let's say I had one or two concerns. Running from A to B? Fine. Figuring out coordinates to find a route with my lot? What could possibly go wrong? I was imagining what might happen, so I said, 'Why don't we stick with cross-country?'

'No, it's fantastic,' replied the drill instructor. 'You'll see who the leaders are, it's brilliant and this is how we do it. They'll love it.'

So, I said OK and let them get on with it. Then I had second thoughts because I had one player under strict curfew. I was responsible for his whereabouts at all times while he was with us, and now he was going to be running loose in the woods in rural Scotland. In truth, I needed to be with him, but there was no way I could do a 10k run at that stage – which is what orienteering equated to – so I decided to pair him with another really smart, young lad who had never put a foot wrong and was the most diligent kid in the world, even if he wasn't the sharpest tool in the box – though I didn't know that at the time.

I honestly couldn't see there being any issues with temporary transfer of care. Orienteering is basically going from checkpoint to checkpoint, and usually about 1.5k into the woods, there would be a unique number that you put into your electronic chip device to confirm you'd been there before getting the next set of coordinates and then having to figure out the quickest way to get to the next checkpoint.

The problem was that a couple of my senior lads, Marc Bircham and Kevin Gallen – two of the craftiest characters you could meet – had paired up and were about to create mayhem. I could see them hatching something as they were about to set off. Gareth Ainsworth had clocked they were up to no good as well and I heard him tell his partner Martin Rowlands that they were going to follow them.

'Oi, what are you up to?' I shouted over to them.

'It's alright, gaffer,' said Gareth, 'we think they might win so we're going to shadow them.'

The instructor got them all into a line and shouted 'go!' and Birch and Gallen sprinted off like bats out of hell and I was thinking, 'Hang about. What's going on here?' They were soon out of sight, following their compass, with Rowlands and Ainsworth desperately trying to keep on their tail.

Everyone else was jogging and laughing at them, saying they couldn't keep that pace up and they'd blow up at some stage. But what none of us knew was Birch and Gallen had sprinted to the first two points and changed the coordinates on the second one – effectively meaning nobody could possibly finish the course because the directions to the third point had been changed and they could never find the fourth checkpoint as a result. Because I'd never done orienteering before, I didn't know it was that easy to cheat – if I had, I would have smelled a rat straight away and probably stationed one of my staff at each point to make sure everything was above board.

My fears grew about an hour later, when in came Bircham and Gallen – who weren't the best runners by any stretch of the imagination – but I just hoped maybe they'd figured out the course better and the others were struggling with the coordinates and compasses.

'You alright?' I said.

'Yeah, yeah, gaffer, all good.'

'You haven't done anything, then?'

'No, nothing, gaffer!'

'Yeah, well it's unusual for you two to be at the front . . .'

We then waited for the others to follow. And waited. And waited . . . Finally, two hours later, a few began returning saying, 'It's impossible gaffer', 'That's rubbish', 'Oh my God!' and suchlike. Four hours had passed when the majority of the squad had returned, but there was still no sign of one pair in particular – and you can probably see where this is going. In Kinloss, it stays grey for most of the day and you have about four hours of good daylight, and it was starting to get dark, so I was starting to panic a bit.

None of the lads were allowed their phones with them, so we were literally in the dark as to where they were – so we had no choice but to inform the emergency services that we'd managed to lose two of my players. We had an air-sea rescue helicopter, police and RAF personnel looking for them. It was like a scene out of *The Fugitive*.

Then we got a phone call to the RAF base. It was a Kinloss resident. 'Just to let you know we saw two lads in QPR track-suits jumping over our back garden fence and we wondered if they belonged to you?'

Thank God they were alive! We set off to try and locate them in the area they'd been reported and we eventually spotted them about two miles away on the edge of a cliff, so we were making our way there when the air-sea rescue called in to say it was OK, they'd picked them both up and it wasn't a problem. When the helicopter landed, they both got out wearing the silver foil sheets you see marathon runners put on after finishing – and I could also see this bright light flashing on one of my lads' right ankle.

'That's it, I'm going to jail. I'm going to jail, I know I am!' he was muttering.

'Don't worry,' Birch chipped in. 'I'll visit you every day.'

It was past curfew so I had to get him into a car, with the officer from the camp, to explain to the local police that we'd lost him while orienteering. The fact was, he very nearly did get taken back to London and put in jail as a result – plus I got a hammering from the police. Eventually, they let us return to the training camp and, thankfully, he would ultimately be cleared of all the charges against him.

The orienteering escapade had taken six hours from start to finish. It goes without saying, I was furious over the whole episode, and seeing that I was on the warpath, Birch and Gallen decided they wouldn't own up to what they'd done and let me think it was just a case of my lads not understanding orienteering. I suspected them, of course, but couldn't prove anything. Two years later, they finally came clean!

On a training camp like that, it's always nice to give the lads the last night out, but when you're in places like Kinloss, there's not much nightlife – in fact, there was none, so there wasn't really anywhere for them to go. The lads and my staff all headed out on the last night in Inverness but were back early and I had to get the RAF base to open up their bar, which my senior players almost drank dry, so one or two of them were worse for wear the following day.

I told them they'd better not be ill on the flight back

to London or they'd be finished with me, because I wasn't having it. I didn't mind them letting their hair down, but what some of them had done had been over the top. Just before we boarded the plane home, we had a team photo on the tarmac and the evidence is there for all to see as one of my senior pros, who was meant to be looking after the younger ones, can be seen throwing up in the background as the picture was taken – on the tarmac of the runway, no less. I made him even sicker later because I fined him when we got home.

So, while I might have had one or two mishaps on pre-season, I think I had it pretty nailed down overall.

Ollie's Tip: You might think you have a great pre-season event planned out, but with footballers around you always need to expect the unexpected.

Tales of the unintentionally ridiculous are legion in pre-season – at least in some of my pre-seasons at QPR.

Case in point: RAF Aylesbury.

I wanted to find the steepest hill possible for resistance training and RAF Aylesbury was perfect because it had a 300-metre high hill covered in sand to make running up really tough because the land was giving way beneath you as you climbed. My plan was for the players to do three runs up the hill and the last leg had to be the fastest. I was really fit at that time, and I knew I could do it, so I showed them how and my final time – because I'm a determined SOB – was as fast if not faster than my first one.

Mentally, it's tough because to begin with, you think 'I'm never going to manage three of those hikes', and the middle one is actually the hardest because you're thinking, 'Christ, I've still got another one to do', but the third one is actually the easiest because you know you just have to give it everything and then you're finished.

The lads absolutely hated me for that run, and they told me it was the hardest thing they ever did. I told the fitness instructor how many runs I wanted them to do, and they said it couldn't be done and that I'd get injuries. I said I didn't care because I was trying to train them mentally and to be able to do something that they didn't even believe was possible. I paid for it later on, because my stomach muscle twisted into a cramped-up knot later that day and I was in absolute agony. Of course, the lads were laughing their heads off. They almost wished it on me! These runs were legendary, and my lads would tell their mates I was a feckin' nutter and a fitness fanatic, but looking back, I think they remember it fondly.

That was one of the things I liked to do with my lads in pre-season, but there were loads of other things at RAF Aylesbury that we did, such as leadership exercises and team-work missions and whatnot, all aimed at sharpening their fitness and building camaraderie.

One involved carrying a life-sized mannequin that was the same weight as a body on a stretcher. That was done in a team of eight, with four carrying the stretcher for a minute at a time, then another four taking over so everyone had equal time. They had to travel over difficult terrain under the orders of the RAF instructors, but some of my lads cheated again and it might come as no surprise to learn that Marc Bircham was involved. Again.

The unit he was in returned to base without the rubber mannequin and the instructor went mental.

'Oh, yeah,' Birch said, 'we decided to leave him behind because he was holding us back. That was my decision.'

'In fairness,' said the instructor, 'it's a good decision, really – but where's the feckin' body?'

Fortunately, Birch had left it somewhere that was easy to find, the clever bastard.

So, we had all these teams bringing back a body on a stretcher and one group says, 'we got rid of the body because he's holding us back.' It was hilarious.

Birch later told me it had been one of the most horrendous pre-seasons ever, with everyone pushed to their limits and even Gareth Ainsworth – who is fit as a fiddle – was throwing up, along with everyone else. I think I got my money's worth out of that visit to an RAF base, but after those successive pre-seasons, we had an opportunity to do some warm-weather training in Ibiza and we were told the facilities at the complex that had been chosen were great and there would also be a tournament – the Ibiza Cup – involving Ibiza Town, Sant Antoni de Portmany FC, and Coventry City, so we'd play a semi-final and a final.

I was assured it would be a fantastic trip that was effectively free, because we had 1,000 or so QPR fans buy into an official travel package that would ensure all our costs were covered. But when we arrived, the facilities were ridiculously bad. There was an Astroturf pitch that was peeling up at the corners and was generally worn and poorly fitted – a carpet laid by a carpenter.

But that was just half of our problems. Because Ibiza is a party island full of partygoers, the lads were constantly asking if they could go out and have some fun. Where we were staying was filled with holidaymakers, so when we went for a run through the streets it was almost impossible to get through, and I spent most of the time fuming that we'd been hoodwinked into believing this would benefit our pre-season.

We did what we could and went into our first game against Ibiza with a good following inside the ground. It was boiling hot, so there were plenty of beers being sunk on the terraces – not a brilliant mix with Brits abroad. Then there was a flashpoint when an Ibiza player took out Paul Furlong with a late challenge. Typical Furs, he got up, brushed himself down and waited for his chance to get some payback. We didn't have to wait too long as he cleaned out the lad with a challenge that

was at least as bad, if not worse, than the one he'd had earlier
... and a twenty-man mass brawl promptly ensued.

So, this is a pre-season friendly where you don't want any
injuries or trouble and the emphasis is supposed to be on
building up match sharpness, and I'm sitting there watching this free-for-all thinking, 'Honestly, what the feckin' hell
is going on?' The fighting on the pitch then spills onto the
terraces and the QPR fans start fighting with the Ibiza fans.
I had to go to the stadium announcer and ask our fans to
calm down on the PA. It was a nightmare. Tommy Doherty,
who I'd only just signed and had a fuse shorter than a candle,
had lost the plot so I had to take him off. My plan of giving
an equal number of minutes to my players quickly fell apart
and I decided I just needed to get us through the game. We
won 2–0 which meant we were in the final against Mickey
Adams' Coventry City a few days later, and I'd always got on
great with Mickey.

We started the game and before I knew what was happening, we were 2–0 down and then the QPR and Coventry
fans began fighting in the stands. It was a joke. So at half-
time, Mickey went on the mic to ask his fans to calm down
and I went on after him to ask our fans to do the same. I said,
'Look, at the minute, we're being beaten by the better team,
but in the second half, we're going to give it a right good
go!' And then everyone started fighting again for about five
minutes.

As it was, we came out and scored three times to win the game 3–2 and clinch the Ibiza Cup. We'd just been taken over by Gianni Paladini's consortium who had taken us out of administration after winning promotion, and this was the first pre-season tour we had done since then, so when we were presented with the cup, I had to do a double-take because it was a replica of the Champions League trophy. Paladini came onto the pitch, and as he was filming himself dancing and celebrating with our fans with this trophy, sending it out to the investors in the consortium, the handle falls off the feckin' cup!

That was the closest either myself or QPR got to the European Cup. Afterwards, I got told off by a police official who said, 'How dare you use that mic to stir up the crowd in that way.' Safe to say, I never returned to Ibiza again, either for pre-season training or to take my family on holiday and I'm not sure they would have let me back in if I had.

Ollie's Tip: If you're going abroad for a training camp, avoid at all costs the place with the all-night clubs and beer-fuelled holidaymakers. You might find some of your own players going AWOL.

After that fiasco, I needed another pre-season training camp and found a place called Cascades in the Valley of the Wolves in Portugal. The pitches were fantastic, and it had the biggest hill I'd ever seen – which made me very happy. It was so good that I used it for the next five years in succession with my various clubs; I took Blackpool, Millwall and Palace there and gradually exorcised the demons of Ibiza in those magnificent surroundings.

What I can say is that I learned when I was a Wimbledon player, from manager Dave Bassett, how *not* to do a pre-season. We were on a golfing trip to Quinta do Lago in the Algarve, and it was absolutely horrendous. It was actually an end of season bash, and everyone was getting arrested and getting into trouble. We were turfed out of our hotel, because one day a load of them had gone out drinking in the morning and by the afternoon, they were firing golf balls at the guy in the crazy golf hut. The police arrived, they threw down their clubs and ran off. Great, so there was camaraderie, togetherness, and team spirit, but with Wimbledon it was always over-exuberance and then some, and their antics convinced me that if I went into management, that was the blueprint for how not to behave aboard, whether on a pre-season training camp or end of season do.

It wasn't just the senior pros like Wally Downes who were leading the chaos, either – it was 'Harry' Bassett too. He wanted them to have 'fun'. But there's a difference between having fun and ruining somebody's holiday. There were fishermen on the docks and when you've got someone diving in, swimming over to their line and coming up with the fish and biting it in half – as John Kay did – it's not the best look, is it? If it'd been John Scales, then maybe.

My ethos for pre-season was to get the players working as hard as possible, get them fit and then reward them at the end. It's always about getting the balance right and staying professional. It was all skew-whiff at Wimbledon and I made sure my own lads stayed within the set parameters on our trips abroad.

5

'Off-piste' Coaching

Life is about your team and your people being
encouraged enough to not be afraid to fail.

One of my most effective 'around the houses' ways of expressing a thought was to a young defender who hadn't played in my first team at QPR. I was watching him play and he was consistently doing the wrong thing.

The goal was behind him, and if the opposition midfielder had the ball and wasn't being pressed, he was anticipating a pass to the centre-forward's feet; but he should have been dropping off because he was making it easy for the midfielder to play it in behind him for the forward to run on to, and on SIX occasions that led to a one-on-one situation against us as the ball kept getting knocked over his head into the space behind.

I hadn't coached him yet, so after the game I went over to him and asked why he continually did the same thing and effectively got caught behind time and time again. He said, 'Oh, that's how I've been coached.' I told him he needed to protect the goal better and he said, 'Yeah, I know – I'm trying to.'

I thought, hang on, he's not getting this. How could I explain that he was inviting trouble every time and that he didn't want the striker having a clear run in on goal?

'OK, you're watching the midfielder who has no pressure on him – and you know the goal is behind you – so let's think about this logically. You want to invite the ball in front of you, but your body position is all wrong and you're making the midfielder's mind up each time by leaving so much space behind for him to play the ball into.'

'Who's your favourite person in the world?' I asked him.

'Oh, my nan.'

'Brilliant,' I said. 'Now we've established that, I'm going to ask you to defend your nan.'

He looked at me, puzzled. 'I don't know what you mean.'

'Look, you're in her house and she has a front door that you're looking at and if someone comes in that front door, you're ready, I know you are. What about the back door? Does she have a back door to her house?'

'Yeah.'

'OK, if you were in her house, you're protecting your nan and she's behind you, but you're only protecting her against somebody coming in the front door. You're not protecting her from somebody coming in the back door. So, I'll put it to you again – if you are protecting your nan and she's right beside you, what would you do?'

He thought about it and said, 'Well, I'd have to get in the middle and get a bit closer to the back door in case they came in that way while watching the front door.'

'Bingo!' I said, 'Exactly. You've been so focused on protecting the front door, you forget about the back one. See what I mean?'

'Oh, yeah . . . I get it. I'm gonna have to drop back a bit, aren't I?'

A couple of weeks later, I saw this kid's dad and he said, 'I thought you were mad when I heard what you told him about his nan's house and the front door and back, but look how he's playing now. Thank you.'

Ollie's Tip: You just have to find a way and the frustrating thing about being a manager is you know exactly how you want your players to play, but they don't. Some of the experienced ones get it straight away, but others don't so you have to find a way of explaining, no matter how you do it because everyone is different, and your job and your duty is to try and make them understand.

You can't have a complete painting because you have to allow for artistic licence and interpretation, but you have to put in the broader brushstrokes and let them fill in the finer detail.

In my younger management years, I'd be giving the players too much info and was too intense and I realised that while they were trying to interpret what I'd said when they played, they were overthinking and not doing what came naturally to them. It's a huge skill that everyone thinks they've got, but you have to assess what you do on a regular basis.

Look at the Romans. In their first battle with the Greeks, they got their asses kicked, they got smashed by the soldiers with the big spears and their shields were too small. They went away with their tails between their legs and changed nearly everything they did, because they knew they wouldn't beat them if they stayed the way they were. They changed the shape and size of their shields; they practised battle strategies by trying new things and tactics, so they weren't as susceptible to the longer spears, they used shorter swords and went back into battle and beat them.

Sound familiar? Sound more than a bit like football management? That's because it is.

Food for thought: I look at being a manager like this – you are the tiny voice on top of a dormant volcano, shouting as loud as you can. But imagine that volcano is the football club – you need to get the volcano to be solid on either side of the peak you're sat on. You're that little ice cap on the peak that should never melt; you should always be there to stop everything erupting all around you and keeping things as cool and under control as possible

The people in charge at the club – the owners, chairman, chief executive and suchlike – they can look at the volcano from any angle they want, but they should never get on your volcano because if they do, they'll slide down the sides and the ice cap will start to melt. If I ever see my chairman hug a player, I ask them please don't do that, because ultimately they are the ones that pay our wages and the ones who might need to make some very tough decisions – and the bottom line is, it undermines the manager.

And here's the craziest thing you've ever heard – PSG allegedly gave a contract to a 23-year-old that included a massive signing-on fee plus – so many news reports suggested – a say in which players they signed and who the manager is! There is something fundamentally wrong with that, isn't there?

You have to speak to your owners and make it clear they must never undermine you while you're trying to build something for them.

But it does happen, and it happened to me at one of my clubs where I had a player come in that I didn't know about, wasn't comfortable with and frankly didn't want.

I needed more firepower, and we had targets in mind – but unbeknown to me, there was an agent who was really close to the chairman, who was throwing names at him and not me.

On this particular occasion, the agent had a player waiting in his car in case the deal we were trying to push through for a player I did want, didn't happen. I wanted Nicklas Bendtner from Arsenal and I'd met him, I liked him and asked him about some of the stuff that had been written about him and for me, he was really focused on his football. I thought he could be a great signing for us, but I'd needed to meet him first. I was thinking he could bring us that little extra bit of quality we needed. I left the ground thinking all that was going to go through, but I came in the following morning and sitting there was another lad.

I called up the chairman and said, 'What's he doing here? I didn't ask to sign him – I knew nothing about him.'

He told me he was only on loan and that the Bendtner deal had fallen through.

'So after all that, you didn't sign him? And you didn't tell me?'

'Something happened at the end, and I wasn't having it. It was late.'

'So you had other plans that I knew nothing about?'

'Ol, what you've got to realise is that it's my show.'

And there it was. The bottom line in management. You, as the manager, believe it's your show, but the truth is it's never your show. It belongs to the owner, chairman and supporters and you'll never be anything other than somebody passing through. It was an important lesson for me and it made me think long and hard.

I asked how was it his show if he was asking me to run it for him? How did that work?

'Ol, we needed one in, and I've got one.'

'No, you're too close to this particular agent,' I said, 'and you've undermined me with him. He hasn't mentioned this player once to me and you probably heard that the kid isn't on my radar.'

He asked what I meant.

'He stands around too much. I spoke to Mick McCarthy about him, and he called him "a stood" – as in "stood still you lazy fucker!" I'm going to have to tell him how I feel.'

So, I went in and spoke to him bluntly and said, 'I didn't know about this deal. I would have you when you used to run around and chase lost causes, but now, I think you think you're too good, you don't want to run around and that ain't any good to me.'

'I've come here to play.'

'You've got to earn the right to play, son,' I said, 'and I'm warning you, if you don't run around like you used to run around when you were a young lad, you won't be playing. You're like a retired racehorse put out to stud, because when you should be chasing lost causes, pressing, and defending from the front, you're just stood around doing nothing! I don't care whether the chairman likes you or whoever else likes you, I need you to do whatever I fucking need you to do, like my other lads have just done. I think you used to do that, but I'm not sure you do anymore.'

His agent was there as well, so I turned to him and said, 'Next time, you tell me what's happening. It's terrible and it's embarrassing, and my chairman should have told me what's happening, but it's your relationship with him that I don't fucking like.'

So, how bad was all that, then?

Ollie's Tip: You have to be prepared to say if a player isn't right for you, no matter how it looks from the outside.

You have to be true to yourself and stick by your principles, no matter what, and that only comes with experience and reputation because if you take that attitude too early in your career, you probably won't have a job for long, either. It's about achieving the right balance with the person you are working with, but that is getting more difficult to do because of chief executives, directors of football and the list goes on and on. If you can't communicate directly with the person you need to be on the same page with at all times, you're in trouble because your relationship has to be spot-on. Or, at worst, it has to be spot-on with the man who has the ear of the king.

In olden times, the person who had the ear of the king was a powerful individual – today, the most influential players have the ear of the king. This is wrong. Owners cannot be connectable to the players and all their bullshit – because that's what it will be. They have to be separate entities. To function properly, that's how it has to be.

That's how I handled it, but my advice would be, I wouldn't do that if I were you!

Don't do it my way, but at the time I couldn't help it. That hurt me so much. I told the chairman that he couldn't do that to me if I was going to work with him, but the golden rule here is that if you fall out with your chairman, there's almost certainly only going to be one winner.

About six days later, I was sacked.

I'd taken it personally, but it had made me think that maybe I couldn't give the club what they needed if they were going to treat me like that. The chairman had asked me to come in and change the way the team played because he was a little bit bored with it, but he'd never told me it was 'his show' and I was beginning to understand why the previous manager had maybe wanted to leave in the first place.

We parted ways with the old 'mutual consent' explanation, but I made a huge mistake, and it was a mistake that was nobody else's fault but mine because I got something drastically wrong.

Without going into too much detail, there'd been talk of a payment when I first signed for the club but I had failed to get it written in the contract and when I was about to leave, I raised the issue about the agreement we'd had which was based on a target I'd achieved and the chairman said, 'Why would I do that now?'

'You would do that because you promised me you would, we shook hands on it and you're a man of your word.'

'That's not a businessman's way of doing it. That's wrong,' he said. 'You should have had that in writing. I'm not going to do it and I'd be stupid to do it. That's your and your agent's fault.'

I told him I had trusted him to do the right thing, but there was nothing I could do and as a result, I had a pittance of a pay-off – and I mean pittance – so he had the funds to get in whoever he liked. But he was right, it was my fault and nobody else's and in business, people don't work on trust – so get your conditions and financials written in concrete or pay the price.

Typical me, I then helped him identify my own replacement because I told him the players would play the way he wanted, and he was the best at it. He took about a month to bring him in, but when he did, it worked really well for them, and he took them up the table fairly quickly.

In fairness to my former chairman, what he's done with the club up to the present day is fantastic, but working his way was not the way I wanted to manage. We'd been good for each other, but it was time to move on.

Improvised training

Improvised training comes at a specific time of the season when you've had a lot of games or you're not getting what you want out of the players.

There's a 'foot off the gas' type of improvisation, but that's something that really only comes with experience. If you're a new manager, you've got a hell of a lot to learn because if you keep at it and at it, and you don't give the players a break or have a change when they're not expecting it, you won't release that pressure. If you want to do well, you have to find ways to vary the routine, because nobody keeps winning all the time and there will be a few bad results or the odd bump in the road – and you don't want that to become a mental problem.

It's all about getting the balance right between your physical output and your mental output, and if you can't just make one day where you take total pressure off the mental side, so they can relax and enjoy themselves, you're in trouble.

It's amazing what that does physically as well, and that's something I've never been afraid to do as a manager because I knew I needed that as a player. If I got too intense, my form would definitely dip, but if I was happy and free and ready to go and I didn't have that mental stress, the difference was quite incredible.

At QPR, Gerry Francis was the only manager I played for who got that absolutely perfectly right for all of us. He was really intense, then he'd have a small-sided game and have a laugh – or make fun of somebody's name in the opposition we had up next. We never stepped over the mark or were complacent because he always got that right, and he was a huge influence for me and how I went on to manage.

It's about understanding how you are yourself as a manager. Nobody is as intense as you – never -- because they're looking for you to lead them. It's all about getting that trigger right and that also means listening to your staff if your own intensity is too much, stepping back if need be and releasing the tension somehow.

I've done hundreds of different things over the years that I believe were circuit-breakers when I felt the stress and pressure was getting too much for my players. What you do can be anything. Paintballing, go-karting, clay pigeon shooting, a poker tournament, a day at the beach where we went in the sea and had ice cream and God knows what else after. There's splash and slide and ballet training; we once went to the cinema; we also watched a movie at the training ground; and we jogged down to the café where I bought them all breakfast and then sent them home – all unexpected and unplanned. Camaraderie is important and doing something together with no pressure is crucial in that.

You also have to be prepared to change your session at the drop of a hat if need be. Those are usually caused by adverse weather conditions. We did that regularly at Blackpool because the strong winds off the Irish Sea would blow the goals around and across the pitch and the players would look like Michael Jackson, walking against the wind, so we had to do different things.

One of the funniest we arranged was a golf day at Blackpool where there was a par three course by the boating lake. A lot of players love golf and are good at it, but there are plenty who can't play, and it was hilarious watching them because they were so bad. Then we went in the boats and the lad who had been the worst at golf got dunked in the water by his teammates and was forever known as 'Digestive' thereafter. I didn't go to that because it's important you give them space and let them hear another voice – my coach Steve Thompson on that occasion. I don't like golf anyway, it always makes me angry, probably because I'm no good at it.

Regularly self-review

Life is always about doing. Are you brave enough to try? And I believe all my players were because I'd convince them they could do it and wouldn't hammer them if they failed. And then it's about being honest when you self-review. Your self-reviewing in anything you do in life is vital. Some people do it in a way where they're never taking enough responsibility, so they're never going to improve. For me, your life is about your team and your people being encouraged enough to not be afraid to fail and then review themselves so brutally and honestly that they see what they do wrong first before they blame someone else.

In management, you try and create an environment where there is a freedom to fail. You don't *want* to fail – the idea of football is not to fail and to win on a regular basis – but you realise it is part of the process so when you do fail, there is no fear attached to it because that paralyses you.

You have to make a fearless environment of learning and growing and appreciating that when it goes wrong, we're going to look at it and take ourselves forward and learn. And that's the hard bit.

When you are managing in a team sport, it's very easy for

it to be all about ME, ME, ME, ME – and it's not. It's about THEM. If you can get that right, through continual assessment, that's when you really can be a manager. And that only comes through experience, getting things wrong and brutally assessing your own performance throughout to be able to go again.

That's why I believe I started to get better results later in my career, because football can be all about egos sometimes, but with management, the last thing you want is your ego in the way.

At every coaching session that you take to get your badges, they should tell you before you start, 'Excuse me, leave your ego at the door before you go in, would you?' You just can't carry that around with you.

I've never really been in a situation where I was expected to win, even in some of my bigger jobs. At QPR, we were in administration, so I had an excuse, didn't I? I was always sitting in the underdog seat: at Palace, it had been a long time since they'd been a force in English football and at Blackpool, nobody expected us to do much when we were promoted to the Premier League. Bristol Rovers were definitely always an underdog, and Plymouth and Millwall – they were never really expected to do anything, were they? So, I suppose I've always been with clubs where expectations were fairly low. Maybe Leicester is the exception because they had lofty ambitions but weren't doing so well at the time.

I always go back to the people who made me want to manage – Bill Shankly and Brian Clough – who could take over something and tell those people where they're going to be and what they're going to be doing, and just do it. 'We're going to get promoted to the top division, then we're going to win that, and then we're going to win the European Cup!' I mean, come on, it's incredible, isn't it?

6

Player Acquisitions

It wasn't long before we had bailiffs turning up at the training ground trying to repossess his car.

Signing players is never straightforward, but there have been some that have been more unusual than others.

I was down at Plymouth as manager when I desperately needed a centre-half. Pen got in touch and said, 'We've got this kid here, we don't know much about him, but I do know he's been released by Heerenveen in the Dutch Eredivisie, and he's played more than a hundred times for them, but now they're letting him go, so he might be trouble – you've got to be good to play for them, so there might not be that many issues. But we can have a look and maybe sign him?'

'Have a look?'

'Yeah, they're happy for him to come over and train with us for a couple of weeks so you can have a proper look at him. See how he trains, see if you like him and we'll be alright – he's bound to be a player.'

'Great,' I said, 'let's get him over.'

It was an odd one for us, because usually Pen knows what the player has for breakfast, dinner and tea and just about everything else there is to know when we are looking at a prospective signing, but he didn't know a thing about this lad. His name was Marcel Seip, and he turned out to be a lovely kid – really nice, quiet and he looked as fit as any butcher's dog I'd ever seen. He was hungry, strong and he looked like a proper athlete who was ready to go.

I couldn't have been happier with him, but when I went into work on the Monday morning after he'd been with us for a week, I got a call from the chairman telling me the police wanted to see me.

'Oh, right. Why's that, then?'

'One of our lads has been involved in a fight,' said the chairman.

'Oh and how many times has that happened down here, then?' I said, thinking of the reputation certain bars in the city had, especially on a Saturday night or if the sailors were in town.

'Quite a few times. But they want to talk to you about it. It's the new triallist we've got.'

I told him not to judge him just yet and that I'd speak with the police to see what they came up with. I went to training first and Marcel was there, so I asked him what happened.

'I was helping out my fellow teammate.'

I asked him who, and he said he didn't want to tell me. I asked him why and he said, 'Well, I don't tell tales on people, but he was in trouble, so I helped him.'

I told him OK, and that the police were coming over to watch CCTV of the incident. They did and they played me the recording of the fight. I could see as clear as a bell that it was a local nightclub and the bouncers were outside when out comes my centre-forward, Sylvain Ebanks-Blake who I'd just signed from Manchester United, followed by two lads who went over and tried to pick on him. And then another of their mates emerged – though he wasn't really involved in the antagonising. It was the other two who started pushing Sylvain around. The bouncers were doing nothing, but thirty seconds later, out comes Marcel Seip who says something to the lads. Sylvain moves out of shot and the three of them turn towards Marcel who, in a blur, knocks out two of them before turning to the third one who runs away.

The bouncers, who'd done fuck-all up to that point, then come over and get hold of Marcel, drag him back inside and call the police. The officer showing me said, 'So, what do you think?'

I asked whether they'd asked Marcel what had happened, and they said they had and that he told them he'd been protecting his teammate, so I said that's what it looked like to me, too. The officer said that he'd badly hurt both lads and that they might want to press charges.

'Why would they? They started it didn't they?'

'Yeah, but not on him,' said the officer.

I told them that's not right, he was protecting Sylvain because the bouncers did nothing, so he stepped in and helped his teammate, which in all honesty is what I would have wanted him to do. I asked the officer what he thought, and he said, 'I think he might be in trouble if they press charges.'

'OK,' I said, 'we'll ask my centre-forward what they said to him and see if they were threatening him, because we might want to press charges against them, first. Let's see what happens.'

So, the chairman looks at me after the police left and says, 'Well, what should we do with him?'

'You know I've been looking for a tough centre-half who looks after his teammates. Me, I would sign him right now. If he'd run away or lost the fight, I probably wouldn't be interested!'

I talked with Marcel afterwards and he explained he used to be a nightclub bouncer – his family owned a nightclub and he also said he always liked boxing so he knew how to look after himself if and when needed. Perfect. I wanted players who would look after their teammates and in the end, we signed him, he was excellent for us, and later on he married the chairman's daughter!

No charges were brought against him and that was the last we heard of it, but I suppose you could claim that I had signed a player based on what I'd seen from a nightclub's CCTV rather than a typical YouTube showreel.

That was a transfer that was unorthodox and an exception to the rule in the way Pen and I vetted players. Was it foolproof? Not entirely, and every now and then, one slipped through the net – but he shall remain nameless.

QPR were due to fly overseas for a pre-season tournament and as we were checking in for the flight, we were told our new signing's passport wasn't valid and that he wouldn't be able to fly.

I asked to look at his passport and I couldn't stop laughing when I saw it. It was sellotaped together with a picture that I swear wasn't his. He'd told us he was 27, but the passport had expired quite a while before and I think his true age must have been about 34! We had to leave him at the airport and fly off without him.

He was probably one of the worst signings I ever made, and it pains me to say that about any footballer. Not long after he arrived at QPR, I got a call from his previous landlady to say he'd left owing numerous bills in his name, though he swore they weren't his – but they had to be as only he'd lived there.

It wasn't long before we had bailiffs turning up at the training ground trying to repossess his car.

He suffered a bad injury towards the end of his time with us and he was at a game at Loftus Road on crutches. Bear in mind he'd only just had an operation, but I was told that after the game, he sprinted quicker than Linford feckin' Christie to get hold of one of his teammates and began beating him up because he'd asked for the money he owed him to be repaid before he left the club. I had to fine him for that, but we made sure we did it at source and took it out of his wages before he could spend it. By that stage, everyone knew we were getting rid of him.

When he'd first arrived, one of my staff had a spare flat that was vacant, so we initially put him there. He stayed there during his time at QPR, but when he left, my member of staff went to clear the flat and clean it ready to be rented out again, only to discover he had left behind a huge photo which was about eight foot by six foot over the fireplace – of himself.

There were final demand letters strewn all over the flat, court summons and Christ knows what else. The only thing he'd opened was his wage packets.

We eventually released him, and I haven't heard of him since.

One of my favourite signings and one that I still con-sider having been a stroke of genius was bringing Sylvain

Ebanks-Blake to Plymouth from Manchester United. Trust me, convincing a young star at one of the biggest clubs in the world to come all the way down to Devon is not easy, but somehow we pulled it off.

My trump card was Gary Penrice, who would be helping to coach him and make him a better striker – and Sylvain's agent was well aware of what we'd done for the likes of Jason Roberts, Nathan Ellington, Jamie Cureton, and Barry Hayles, among others – so we had that in our favour, but the logistics of him coming to Plymouth from Manchester were a bit difficult. Plus, there were other clubs after him, too, including Wolves, who were probably just an hour away from where he lived.

We had one shot at getting him on board, and to this day I still feel that it was the best bit of management I ever did. The key was to make the lad feel important and wanted, so I went around every member of staff at the club and told them he'd be coming to have a look around and when he did, to call him by his name – 'Hello Sylvain, how are you? Hope you come and join us' – all aimed at making him feel respected and that we knew who he was and where he was from.

I explained to them all that it wasn't nailed on by any means, but if they all did their bit we would have a chance and they went with it.

I also got a No 9 Argyle shirt with his name printed on the back and had it framed. The chairman said, 'Well, what if he doesn't sign?' and I just said I didn't care and to get it done and that it would come out of my pocket.

He wasn't getting any game time at United, so seeing that shirt showed him what it would be like to be a first-choice striker and the No 9 at a club who really valued him. I couldn't impress him with the training ground or our facilities – not when he's coming from Man United – but I could make sure he felt wanted.

As we went around Home Park, the staff were fantastic and everyone he passed said something along the lines of, 'Good morning, Sylvain – how are you?' and he looked taken aback by it all, if I'm honest. Then we presented him with the framed shirt in the club shop, he had a smile as wide as the Tamar Bridge.

It worked, too. We managed to get him for £200,000 and he was fantastic for us, so much so that Wolves came back for his signature two years later, activating a £1.5 million buyout clause in his contract after 74 games and 23 goals for Argyle.

If that was one of the deals I am most proud of, nicking Nathan Ellington from under the noses of QPR while I was Rovers boss is probably one of the funniest. Pen and I had heard about this young kid who was playing for Walton & Hersham in Surrey. We were like Hinge and Bracket (or maybe Starsky & Hutch?) that afternoon when we went to see him play. My wife Kim was sitting with me, and she said, 'Oh, he's brilliant, isn't he?' I asked who was. She said, 'The

No 10' – Nathan Ellington. At half-time I went to see the chairman and said, 'Right, we'll do the deal for £150,000 – let's do it'.

The chairman said, 'You'll have to convince his mum first because QPR want him as well.'

I said that was fine and to leave it to me, then went back out to see Pen climbing up the side of the stand! He told me he wanted to stay incognito and go and mingle with the fans and ask them a few questions about Nathan – but he'd obviously seen enough and was trying to get back to where I was sitting. I spotted him and he was waving his little hand shouting, 'Ol, you've gotta sign him! He's feckin' brilliant – and he's younger than we thought!'

I shouted back that we'd already done a deal.

Pen had discovered by talking to one of the fans that Nathan had been playing under his brother's name and he was actually only 17. I told him it was all done and dusted, apart from convincing Nathan's mum, which we did when they came to look around.

I picked her and Nathan up at the train station and took them to the digs to meet the family he'd be staying with. Then I took them to the training ground and went into the gym and showed Nathan the Olympic weight programme we had planned for him to build up his strength. I told his mum that he'd be in and around the starting eleven because even at 17, I thought he was good enough to put him straight in and not have to start off at academy level. We showed that we genuinely cared, and it all seemed to hit the spot, she trusted us and agreed he should come and play for Bristol Rovers. These were just some of the things we had to do to bring players to what I guess others would call the more unfashionable clubs.

Ollie's Tip: If you don't have much money and the agents aren't going to get what they see as a worthwhile cut, you have to be a bit more creative with how you convince players to sign and get deals across the line.

I think Pen and I mastered that art over time.

Management bugbears: Christmas, Bah, humbug!

Football and Christmas do not go together – at least if you are the one having to play or manage.

As a player, I honestly hated playing over Christmas and when I moved into management, nothing changed. I really didn't like cramming so many matches in over a very short period, but I'm told families enjoy the festive fixtures. Mine didn't!

Going back maybe fifty years, there was more sense to Christmas fixtures, with teams playing local derbies and so there wouldn't be that much travel involved – that was more acceptable – but today, you can end up going anywhere and everywhere.

I remember once when I was playing for Gerry Francis at QPR, we travelled up to Stoke on Christmas Day, so we had to rush opening the presents so I could get to the ground and onto the coach and stayed in a hotel only for our Boxing Day fixture to be snowed off. So, that was Christmas cancelled for everyone and for somebody who loved his kids and wanted to be with them, it always left a bad taste in my mouth.

Another time at Rovers, Gerry had us in for a small-sided game on Christmas Day, and he was having to drive up from London – it's madness, isn't it? It was definitely harder for me when I was playing and my kids were young and you can never get those days and special moments back, because when you try and have an alternative family Christmas Day, it's not the same, is it? I wanted to be there watching their faces as it all happened because I get great joy out of that, and too many times in my career, I wasn't able to do it.

Twice as a manager at Millwall and QPR, we had Norwich City away on Boxing Day – not exactly a local derby. I believe the number of police officers needed if they do play local derbies is too expensive on bank holidays, so that's a factor in the decision-making, but none of it is right. I'd rather be sitting at home on Boxing Day, watching the kids play with the toys Santa brought them, watching repeats on TV, eating too much, and having a drink or two.

So, I would cancel Christmas football and introduce a winter break – bah, humbug – but I don't want to end up like The Grinch. I love the colour of Christmas – the gold, red and green – I love to see the people's faces when they open their gifts and it's a day of joy for me that football probably ruined for forty years or more.

As a manager, I tried absolutely everything to make it better for my lads and their families. We've had Christmas meals together the day before, worst Christmas jumper competitions, I'd buy my players a bottle of wine or something – did they really appreciate it? I'm not sure. At QPR, my staff and I would exchange gifts and it was always a bottle of wine so in the end, I said why don't we just buy ourselves a bottle of our favourite wine and have done with it?

Once, at Bristol Rovers, I gave them Christmas Day off, but we played on Boxing Day, and we were absolutely horrendous. I'd trusted them but they'd probably eaten too much and drank too much, and I felt they'd let me down.

It might have just been coincidental and been a bad performance, but it just didn't feel right, and I never did that again. I know it's an occupational hazard, but I'd like to tell the world that I genuinely hated playing football at Christmas. There are too many games crammed together in a short period and it's just madness.

Player Acquisitions

We all work hard enough, and I think everyone deserves a couple of days with their family over Christmas and it's something I've had a bee in my bonnet about for a fair old few years. Will it ever change? I doubt it.

7

Picking Your Starting XI – and dealing with the fallout

You just have to pick the team you think is going to win you the match . . . you don't owe anyone for playing well – that's what you pay them for.

Picking your starting XI ahead of a game was something of a trial and error process that I probably didn't get right until the end of my career.

By that point, I named my team on a Thursday – if at all possible – along with the tactics and how we were going to approach the game. I did that because when I was a player I had wanted to know as early on as possible because it gives you an extra day to deal with it and get your mind right.

In my playing career, I never really moaned about team selection, and there's only one occasion I can think of when I thought I'd been treated unfairly; but as time went on, I realised that football isn't about fairness and getting in the team isn't about whether you deserve it or not – it's about what the manager thinks.

At QPR, I was playing really well alongside Simon Barker who scored about seven goals during a particular period, but when Ray Wilkins was fit again, it was me that had to make way when I had actually expected to carry on playing. So, Gerry Francis played Ray alongside Simon instead of me and I got the raving hump about it.

At the next training session, I said to Razor, 'I'm gonna kick you, today.'

He just laughed. 'Go on, then,' he said. 'You try it.'

I didn't get anywhere near him. He knew I was coming for him, so he was four passes ahead of me each time. We were playing eleven-a-side and I was trying my best to get to him, but at one point he called for the ball when I was near him, played it back to where it came from and then asked for it to be played into space the other side of me. He laughed at the end, and I said, 'Christ, I didn't get anywhere near you.'

'No, because I knew you were coming, I knew I could play it back to him, drag you in and then tell him where to play it while you're still coming in after me, and then I spin off you and collect it the other side.'

He'd reeled me in, hook, line and sinker!

He continued, 'If I hadn't known you were coming in for me to kick me, I couldn't have done it, could I? So, thanks for helping me play better. It's called lending the ball, and how many times can you do it? You could play that way because you're good enough to do it. You're good enough to think like that.'

After that, I started to do it as well, and at least I got a footballing lesson there. But do you know what I took most from that moment when I found out I wasn't playing? It was how to better understand not being selected and then make sure nobody else felt that way when I became a manager when I told my players about the team selection.

It's natural not to be happy when you've not been picked, and you don't want them to be happy, but you also don't want them to be moaning and whingeing, because it's about the team and not individuals. One thing I said when I went to each of my clubs is that I was going to tell the truth whether the players wanted to hear it or not, and if you want to know why you're not playing, come and see me on the day you find out.

At first, you didn't know how they would react. At QPR, one lad was probably the worst because he wanted to play so badly and he said, 'You like the other lad more than me and you don't like the way I train', and he was constantly moaning. Some players are like that. I didn't like moaners, so I tried to combat it by saying that I didn't want them moaning, come and see me and I'd give them the truth – and then tell them to make sure they were right on Friday, because we were preparing for a match and how could they prepare for the match if they had the raving hump? And if the player they were in direct competition with saw they had the raving hump, they might take that personally, so how can we be a team if that happens? So, let's deal with it and get on with it – and at the end of the day, the players understood that I wasn't putting up with any crap or negativity. I also think they appreciated the fact that I told them as early as possible so they could get prepared.

The physical process I use for selecting the starting XI is a box of magnetic names that you can attach to a board and then move around. You'll have your whole squad, and you'll start with your injured players, so you put them together at the side, then you can see who you have left and pick your team from them.

I've picked teams on a notepad at home, scribbling, crossing out and driving myself mad. Sometimes it's really difficult. In fact, it once got so bad that I called up Graham Taylor, who was always on hand if I ever needed any advice.

'Graham, I get so indecisive sometimes.'

'Son, we all do,' he said. 'Let me tell you the truth. I go with my gut. I've written out the team and handed it out to my staff and then when I go into the dressing room before a game, I sometimes call out a different eleven because I'm the manager and I can do what I like and it felt right to change it, so I changed it then and there and we had to rewrite it to hand into the referee. We all do it and it's just part of being a manager – it's not easy to make your mind up, without the benefit of hindsight, is it? Don't feel you're any less of a manager, because we all do it.'

'Harry' Bassett taught me a valuable lesson at Wimbledon when he told me that you just have to pick the team you think is going to win you the match and said you don't owe anyone for playing well – that's what you pay them for. He added that you can't play the same way against different opposition because it doesn't work and sometimes you have to pick horses for courses.

You have to find your own way of doing things, but the hardest thing of all is telling a player something that they don't want to hear. You want them to be professional and take it the right way, but you don't want them to be happy about it either, so finding the balance of when you tell them is not easy.

It's even harder for someone like me because I get a lot of pleasure out of pleasing people and making them happy. The truth is, for a professional footballer, not being picked is an occupational hazard, like being injured, so my message to anyone who has a strop about not being selected would be to stop being childish and be professional.

Ollie's Tip: I judge players by one mantra – what are they like when they don't get what they want? That's a big question I ask when I am about to sign someone.

'Tell me what he's like when he doesn't get what he wants. Does he sulk? Does he moan? Does he throw his toys out of the pram? Does he get more determined? Does he get angry? Does he blame other people? Or is he a good, strong character who is ready to keep going no matter what?' I'd ask my scouts to try and notice that by watching what they're like if they get subbed. What's their temperament like?

At QPR, I had my first-choice full-backs – Gino Padula and Matty Rose – both injured on the run up to the play-off final and the two lads who came in, Tommy Williams and Terrell Forbes, were fantastic. But I felt I needed to go with my strongest side in the final, so I called all four of them into my office. I said, 'You two have been brilliant (Williams and Forbes), but I'm going back to these two for the final because they've been in for most of the season' – and they accepted it brilliantly. It was the first time I'd ever done that, but it worked a treat.

Over time I discovered that sitting down and having a talk about why a player's not been picked is much more productive than keeping schtum and letting any resentment fester and grow.

8

Fielding a Weakened Team
(even when it isn't)

I actually got dragged in front of an FA panel,
and worse still, they fined me twenty-five thousand
feckin' pounds!

This is the madness of football. I've probably never felt so much injustice in my life.

The season Blackpool won promotion to the Premier League was the first time clubs had been asked to submit a twenty-five-man squad list. If you had twenty-seven, you'd have to leave two off, so you left your younger ones off the list as they were classed as homegrown, and I managed to find twenty-five names to submit to the FA.

Once you've sent it in, it's either approved with a tick or rejected with a cross, so they ticked 'approved' for my list and returned it to me, as they probably did for every club. As far as I was concerned, that was that and I didn't think they could then look at who you picked and criticise.

My question is: how do they know how good your twenty-five-man list is? So, if I choose eleven players from that twenty-five-man list and put some that play more regularly on the bench, shouldn't that be my call?

Would someone then decide that I had fielded a weakened team when that person hadn't been to see my team train or seen my team play on a regular basis? How can they deem that I should be fined as a result? They couldn't', surely? Yet, that's exactly what happened.

So, how did this all come about?

I looked at the games we had coming up and the games we had already played and then had a look at my players' condition, and because the eleven behind the regular starters were training so well – and if anything better than the eleven in front of them at the time – it was with some justification that I was thinking of giving them some much-needed game time.

In the session before the game in question, I played the regulars against the 'second' eleven, and the seconds were beating the firsts – and doing it on more than one occasion. I think they'd earned the right to play, and I had every confidence they'd do just as good a job for me.

I believed that if I started them against Aston Villa away, I could play the other eleven against Spurs a few days later. The lads had done ever so well for me at the start of that season but were looking jaded physically and mentally by their early exertions. We were only eleven games in, but by doing that, they could recharge their batteries and take a well-earned rest – but I'd still keep most of them on the bench in case I needed them.

What the lads who weren't playing that much had shown me on the training pitch was, to my mind, good enough to go to Aston Villa and win. If I did one thing wrong, it was not leaving Charlie Adam in the starting XI because I believe that if Charlie – my talisman – had started along with the second lot of first-team players, I'd have been alright. Because he didn't start, they deemed my team to be too weak.

The truth was my lads were outstanding at Villa Park – and that performance should have been the basis of any judgements made on my selection.

Ludovic Sylvestre was magnificent that night, but he played in Charlie Adam's position, so he hardly ever got a look-in. But oh, my goodness, what a player.

We were fantastic and with minutes to go, we were 2–2 with Villa when Ian Evatt – one of my first-team regulars – came on and he made a mistake that cost us a goal and we lost 3–2. We didn't lose 5–0 at Villa. We didn't lose 8–0. We lost 3–2 with the last kick of the game. How can that be deemed bringing the game into some kind of disrepute?

Was it because we were Blackpool and therefore our second eleven was that much worse than that of Manchester United, Arsenal or Manchester City? I actually got dragged in front of an FA panel, and worse still, they fined me twenty-five thousand feckin' pounds! Me, personally – not the club. Luckily, my chairman Karl Oyston didn't agree with the decision and paid it for me and not out of my wages. But twenty-five feckin' grand!?

And it almost led to me falling out with Mick McCarthy, because I said in my post-match interview that it was OK for Mick to make wholesale changes and he called me up and said, 'Why are you trying to get me into trouble, you pillock?

I said I wasn't and tried to explain and he just said, 'Well don't! Fuck off!'

I told the FA I had rested my main team and played a team I felt were good enough to win and I was almost proved right.

And as for the game against Tottenham a few days later? We beat them 3–1 and my lads were fresh and ready to go . . . but we missed staying up by one point at the end of the season. Was it down to that defeat at Villa? I don't think it was.

If I'm allowed to put a twenty-five-man squad into the FA and they approve those twenty-five players, then surely I'm allowed to pick whoever I like whenever I want from that list?

I'm still fuming about that now because I'm the only manager who ever got fined for fielding a so-called weakened team. I look at the team Jürgen Klopp put out for the Carabao Cup for most of the run they had in 2021/22 – and they ended up winning it – but if he hadn't, would he have been wrong for selecting that side? Would he have been fined? Never!

Arsène Wenger treated the League Cup as a chance to play his youth team (almost), but again, no fines there.

They presumed they knew what my best side was and presumed I deliberately selected a weakened team, but they were wrong. Why would I ever do that?

Food for thought: I didn't break any rules and if I'm honest, I'd still like some answers for what happened. It still doesn't make any sense to me, and I still stand by what I did that night because we played so well.

And yes, I'm still the only manager to ever have been fined for that reason!

What the FA should have done was tell me, 'actually twelve of those players weren't good enough' when we submitted the paperwork, or at least shown me the rule saying I couldn't pick any of those twenty-five players whenever I wanted.

I didn't break any rules and can only think somebody had it in for me (see the chapter on referees).

In for me, in for me . . . boy did they have it in for me!

9

Management Myths: Part 1

*Would a manager really pick a player just because
he liked them as a person?*

Football is for men only

Women's football seems to be heading to a wonderful place, particularly in this country. I watched the Euros in the summer of 2022, and it was fantastic to see the whole country get behind the team, with record-breaking live audiences both in the stadiums and on TV. With the women's game going fully professional and the crowds buying into it, it is just a joy to witness and I'm very proud of them all.

Yet I watched an advert on TV with some of the men's England players talking about sexism in the game and how degrading some of the comments on social media were and I was thinking, 'what, really?'

What is wrong with some people? If young girls have aspirations to play football and earn a living from it, that is fantastic and it should be embraced by all.

England women's head coach Sarina Wiegman has been telling her players that every day in every way, they can get better – a mantra of my managerial career – and she's done a brilliant job. Our England women maybe in the past didn't believe they were good enough to win the Euros, but they do now!

Anyone can play this wonderful game and all the young girls who watched that tournament could do what England did in 2022, if they are dedicated and determined. And they will be able to earn a good living out of it. So why don't you do it and make us all proud all over again? It was so refreshing seeing the families and kids go into the stadiums safely, have fun and not have to deal with the thuggery we often see in the men's game. It's like a bloody big fairy tale unravelling before our eyes and let's hope the performances of our women rub off on the men's team – and for the record, I think Gareth Southgate has done a wonderful job and I hope the fans get behind him, because how can getting England to a World Cup semi-final and a European Championship final be considered a failure?

The game is for everyone and I couldn't be prouder of what our women achieved in the summer of 2022.

The caretaker manager

I've never been a caretaker manager and I've never played under a caretaker manager, either.

When I first started in management, I think managers were a lot more secure in their roles than they are today, and in recent years there have been some really odd situations and decisions made. Take towards the end of 2021/22 when Burnley sacked Sean Dyche and then replaced him with a caretaker manager until the end of the season. To me, that was madness.

People claim that some managers 'lose the dressing room', but that's not something I've ever believed. Sometimes a change is needed because a manager has had enough and doesn't want to do it anymore and a new man may bring a fresh outlook. Chris Hughton is a great manager, but look what Steve Cooper did when he took over from him at Nottingham Forest, which was quite amazing.

But my honest thoughts on caretakers is that clubs shouldn't do it. I think you have to give somebody the job, not wait and see how they get on – you have to commit and say this is who we want, and this is how we'll do it.

Of course, for some, taking on a caretaker role might be the only stab they get at a decent job – and if they do get good results, it might end up in a permanent appointment

– so I understand when members of the backroom staff or Academy coaches snatch at the opportunity. But if I was running a football club, it wouldn't be something I'd ever look to do.

Take the case of Duncan Ferguson at Everton. Having walked in the shoes of a manager and had a taste of it, he's decided that's what he wants to do because he did ever so well as a caretaker but didn't get the job.

I think it's very confusing for supporters, staff and particularly the players. To me, it's a no-no.

In 2021, Barrow in League Two asked me to step in as they were going to get rid of their manager. I told them to keep him, but they went ahead and sacked him anyway, and Phil Brown took it on a short-term basis. I didn't agree with it, and I didn't want to do that – they either wanted me or they didn't.

At Charlton Athletic, Johnnie Jackson was given the caretaker role for one game – which he won – before they brought in somebody on a permanent basis. Then, six months later, they turned to him again and this time he had two months as caretaker, winning nine of thirteen games. They had to give him the job after that, but instead of letting him have a proper transfer window and a full pre-season, they got rid of him before the end of the 2021/22 season – far too soon for a manager who had a total win ratio just shy of fifty per cent.

At the time of writing, he had taken on the AFC Wimbledon job and hopefully, they'll give him the time he needs.

How can anyone buy into what you're saying and believe in your vision when you're only going to be there for a matter of weeks or maybe a couple of months? And in that role, surely everyone is just waiting for that one bad result and it's like, 'oh, here we go' and 'the guy obviously isn't up to the task' – which is bollocks. There just isn't time to buy into the club's philosophy and at the back of everyone's minds is the fact that the caretaker is only patching over until the new manager is installed.

It's a modern-day short fix and I'm dead against it. I don't believe it works on any level whatsoever.

Do managers ask other managers how to beat another team?

Does it happen? I'm not sure that it really does because at the end of the day, it's dog eat dog, and sooner or later, you could be facing the manager who has explained how they managed to beat a team that you might be asking advice on. You get what I mean, don't you?

I've spoken to friends in the game on occasion and asked things like, 'How did you manage that, then?' But basically we are all in competition with each other and obviously your ego won't really allow it because if you do seek advice, it sounds like you don't really know what you're doing.

Plus, everybody has a totally different idea of how to play and we've got totally different players, so it's a bit of a minefield.

People outside the game think all of us managers get on, but we don't share information – even if you're on a course with someone or at a luncheon of some kind, you don't share knowledge or talk about what you do and why, because it's actually a very personal thing. It just wouldn't work and isn't practical.

Are footballers superstitious?

I honestly think there's a bit of OCD in all of us. I've never really had anyone I had to pull up and say, 'look, you're getting this all wrong'. It was probably more the ones who had no preparation or routine that were likely to rile me, because I don't get that.

I used to overthink as a player, until my kids came along, and I started having hardly any sleep.

One thing I used to do was make cups of tea for everyone before the game and from the moment I put the kettle on, I had to get all the teabags in the cups plus the milk and the sugar before the kettle boiled or else I thought we wouldn't win that day.

I had to pull myself up on that because it cannot be linked to that – it just can't! But your mind and your nerves make you feel that way.

I've had a lot of players who wanted to wear a specific number and I asked them, 'Can't you play without that number on your back, then?'

Because I was the way I was, I sort of understood it and tried to give them the number they wanted, but often it meant playing in one they weren't happy with.

When squad numbers came in, it was much easier, but there was still a reluctance to wear No 12, 13 or 14 because that was associated with being a sub when we had fourteen-man matchday squads. Nowadays, those numbers don't mean a thing.

I've experienced players who've said that they need to do this or that and I've just gone with it, because you can very rarely change something that someone does if it means they think they're going to play well.

In short, if they wanted to play with one sock inside out and the other not, be the last out of the tunnel or God knows what, I just let them get on with it.

Do managers have favourites?

Would a manager really pick a player just because he liked them as a person over what they did on the pitch?

We've all heard about players who supporters think are in the team week in, week out, not on merit but because they are a manager's favourite, but it's not an accusation I've ever had laid on me. If there is a situation like that anywhere, I'd suggest that fans aren't giving that manager the credit he deserves because it's likely they are selected for many reasons, and one is what they do every day – the stuff that doesn't get seen. That kind of accusation really annoys me, because does anybody really think a player would be selected because of favouritism? Some managers have the luxury of having an experienced pro in their team just to show the others how to behave. Even dog trainers do it, with an older dog helping young puppies. That's not favouritism, it's just a particular style of management.

If fans think a manager shouldn't be picking someone, I'd ask them to think again because unless you are privy to what they see every minute of every day, and what they are trying to build, you couldn't surely think that any manager would pick somebody on any basis other than merit? Some of these lads might not be the best players, but they might be leaders, or somebody who holds everything together when things are falling apart. It's a nonsensical theory, because we all want to win and to do that, we pick our best players and players we trust.

I think Sir Alex Ferguson liked Ole Gunnar Solskjaer so much because he was always ready to play, whether he picked him or not, and was always professional. Maybe he was Fergie's favourite. Life's about attitude and if anyone wants to know the secret of being successful and having a successful team, you have to find people with the right attitude and application.

But managers' favourites? I'm not having that.

Sacked in the morning . . .

'Sacked in the morning' – a chant no manager wants to hear. It's disgraceful and disrespectful and if it's being sung by your own fans, there's every chance it's going to become a reality.

It only happened to me once, at Millwall, and once is enough for any manager, believe me.

So, where did it all go wrong?

I arrived at Millwall and told the press I was honoured to be their next manager – and I was.

I managed to keep Millwall up in my first season, but the expectation levels the season after didn't match the tiny budget I was left with to strengthen the squad. Starting the new season so well actually didn't help, either, because after five games we were in a play-off spot, but we couldn't sustain that with the personnel we had. Expectation turned to disappointment, then disillusionment and finally moans and when my chairman put out a statement telling everyone he had the highest-paid manager he'd ever had – me – he absolutely killed me stone dead.

The Millwall fans hated that more than anything and all their spew and vitriol was suddenly directed at me. For what was my last game, what I call 'the wrong 'uns' were at the ground in force and when what had been 1–1 turned to 4–1 to our opponents, they were all there around the tunnel, shouting and screaming at me at the final whistle. It is what it is, and I knew what was coming, so there wasn't much I could do to stop it.

With stuff like that, a negative momentum builds up that is almost impossible to stop and there's only one possible outcome – you get sacked, and it's not always in the morning I'd just like to add.

Millwall had a former club legend waiting in the wings in the form of Neil Harris and in all honesty, they were better off giving it to him, but they still got the raving hump because I didn't take them down and that would have made it a hell of a lot easier for them to unleash that hatred, which it had by then become.

I don't blame them, but truthfully, I didn't like what some of them represented. As I say, they had wrong 'uns among their number and when we played Rotherham United away, there was fighting in the crowd and a bloke in the home stand behind me shouted to me, 'Holloway! Your name's all over that because you work for them, so you must agree with it!'

And he was right about the first part: I was employed by Millwall FC. But he was completely wrong about the second part: it went against everything I stood for.

I'd never even thought about it that way before. And I hated it, because that thug element – and it is only the thug element I am talking about – has nothing to do with football as far as I'm concerned. And if you hurt someone in football's name, you're a disgrace.

I was wondering how I could work for Millwall knowing that some of their fans did that? That guy at Rotherham had a point and I honestly couldn't argue with him. I went home and it actually changed the way I thought about what I was doing.

I thought the Millwall fans were passionate about their club – and a lot of them are passionate and care deeply – but it was that small minority that I couldn't stomach, so I started saying as much publicly in the press, that it was wrong, and we shouldn't have it, or do this or that – and by doing so, it was open season and they turned on me.

I've got no issue with it, but I was still right to have said what I said and in hindsight, I should never have taken their job, because deep down, thugs at football matches where families and kids are present, isn't right and never will be. I don't believe in violence. I believe in banter, having a laugh whenever possible and football people taking each other on and having a sporting contest and then congratulating the opponent if they've won and deserved it – not fighting because you wear a different club colour.

Let's be honest, Millwall are not the only club with that element – every club in the land has an element they'd rather not have. It's part of our society that we have to face up to and unless you tell them they're wrong and try and do something about it, it will continue to happen.

I honestly thought I could change how Millwall FC, and their supporters were portrayed, because I wanted to tap into their passion and my passion and channel that in a positive way. But however small that minority of Millwall fans is, it is still obvious, influential and exists.

And I didn't agree with it, so why was I working there? You like to think the way your team plays is a reflection of your own personality and beliefs, and you like to think the way your football club is represents you. The irony is they had tried to get me to be their manager three times previously, and each time they came back with a better offer; in the end, it was too good an offer to refuse. I felt wanted, flattered and maybe for the first time in my life, I took the money. And ultimately, that's what they hated me for, but that's just foot-ball, sometimes, isn't it?

To summarise, I have no problem going to Millwall and being among the ninety-nine per cent of their wonderful fans; it's just that one per cent – and they know who I'm talking about – that I don't agree with.

Parking the bus

Parking the bus. This is something I think every club outside the top six in the Premier League was doing for a while. It's a skill to get a team to defend like that, but it's not something I'd want to watch – and almost every team that plays Man City, apart from Liverpool, parks the bus because they would murder you otherwise.

I saw Chelsea win the Champions League under Roberto Di Matteo playing that way, beating a Barcelona side in the final who hit the bar, hit the post, and missed a penalty before Fernando Torres broke through and scored at the other end. So even the best can play that way and get a result – Jose Mourinho was brilliant at it.

You have to have a team structure and a way of defending to park the bus, and if you look at basketball – when a player has a shot and then they all run back and make a defensive ring around their hoop – that's all it really is. Getting back in numbers, playing safe and getting your defensive lines in place can be very effective if you have a counter-attacking team, but it is not something I'd enjoy coaching and, because it wouldn't float my boat enough, I'm not sure I'd do it very well.

But I do admire teams that can do it, and most champions can defend really well too, but my style was 'attack is the best form of defence' and that's what I wanted my teams to do – constantly attack. Maybe at Blackpool, my team wasn't good enough to do that against the Premier League teams for a whole season, but we had a right good go at it. In the end, I couldn't change it after I'd coached the players to do that week in, week out.

If parking the bus becomes your whole way of playing, I don't like that.

Palace were great at it – not having the ball and counter-attacking – and that was their style when they got promoted. I tried to change it and it didn't work, so I had to go back and play to my players' strength and accept the fact that they were much happier not having the ball. They felt it suited them to play the way their old manager wanted, so it's something I've experienced, but it's not something I really wanted to do.

Parking the bus was popular for a time, but football today is changing. It's not just about winning, but how you win, and the best managers in the world – Pep Guardiola and Jürgen Klopp in particular – are changing the way football is played totally and utterly because fans whose teams don't play that way, don't really like it.

Managers are judged because fans want their sides to play like Man City and Liverpool and if they don't, supporters are asking, 'Why can't we play entertaining, attacking football? Why don't we play like that?' That's what almost everyone wants to see now and if you're a manager who doesn't have your team playing that way, you're labelled as a dinosaur, which I don't think is true, but it all goes round.

At the end of the day, there's lots of different ways to win, and I admire all of them and there is something joyful in getting a team of lads to understand that playing without the ball is their strength, and that's a skill as well.

Having reluctantly done it at Palace, I fully understand it, but would I want to do it if I ever returned to management? Probably not.

Managers' notebooks

One thing that really annoys me, and something that other managers do, is writing stuff down in a notebook. I don't get it. Because as you're doing that, what might you be missing? Why not remember it and keep your eyes on the game?

If it were me, I'd tell one of my coaches or physios to remember something and that would be that.

I see Brendan Rodgers scribbling on bits of paper and if I'm honest, it grinds my gears – and he writes it in Spanish so nobody can else read it! That's just showing off, isn't it?

That never worked for me. I discovered that if you made any more than three points about the performance at half-time, you'd lose the players, and the longer I went on and the more experienced I became, the more specific I made those points. In the past I'd had a habit of flitting from one thing to another when I was excited, and while some enjoyed that enthusiasm, you'll lose people if you don't keep your focus on the main issues.

So, when I see people scribbling notes down now, I think, 'What are you doing that for? Is it for show?' Making public shows is not my style and that puts me in mind of Phil Brown's half-time team-talk with Hull City on the pitch away to Manchester City. You remember, he got them all in a circle and sat them down like kids at nursery while he remonstrated with them in front of a full stadium. Given the chance, I don't think he'd do that again, but he'd probably lost his way at that point.

Jimmy Bullard was hilarious the season after when he scored against City and his teammates sat down with Bullard reprising Brown's role by remonstrating with them, but my point is that you keep some things private, especially a team bollocking.

It's not that I use industrial language I don't want people to hear, it's just that it's us in there – nobody else, just us – that's what we do. I don't get all these behind-the-scenes documentaries where cameras are allowed in the dressing rooms. I don't like it and it's never felt right.

They tried the behind-the-scenes stuff at Palace, and I said, 'No way, it's never going to happen. You don't come into my dressing room unless you play for me – and that's your privilege to come in and listen to what I've got to say. I'm not saying it's a privilege to listen to me, it could well be a feckin' curse depending on what I've got to say. What I'm saying is, it's for us only.'

I have done other things and brought in motivational speakers and other pre-match stuff when I felt it was needed. At QPR, we'd lost our penultimate game of the season so couldn't be promoted as champions. I wanted my players to get over the line in our last game away to Sheffield Wednesday to clinch that final automatic promotion spot and was wondering about what I was going to say ahead of the game.

I bumped into some of our fans at the hotel and they were saying stuff like, 'It doesn't matter what happens today, the boys have been fantastic,' and I thought, 'Wow, the lads need to hear this.' So, I gathered the team in the foyer of the hotel we were staying in and asked about twenty of our fans to come along, and before I said what I wanted to say, I asked the supporters to tell the players what they'd told me earlier.

Between them they said, 'Lads, it doesn't matter what happens today, we're really proud of you and thanks for all your effort this season,' and it took the pressure off them, I thought. Then I said to the team: 'You deserve to get over the line and these fans believe that too – and for what you have done for them and the effort you have given me, I believe we'll do it.'

So, I used our fans' positivity and support to help me do a speech, because I felt it was right at the time. We won 3–1 and got promoted, and I think that helped.

At Blackpool, we had one game left at home to Bristol City knowing that we had to match Swansea City's result to finish sixth and guarantee a Championship play-off spot. We were a point ahead of them, so I decided to ask the players who had brought family members, kids, wives – everybody – with them, to get them all to come into the dressing room before kick-off.

It was just a spur of the moment whim, and it felt right, but Christ, there was loads of them! I asked them all to sit down wherever they could and said, 'Lads, can you all come and stand with me.'

They gathered around me and we were looking at the family members and I said, 'That's what we've got to do – that's who we're doing it for, not to have a bit of fame or whatever, but to have a chance to step up the ladder and earn the promotion bonus that you lot deserve – that *he* should give you (referring to the chairman). Your family is what you're doing it for and I want you to be recognised and remembered in years to come because you've achieved something for this club. On all the walls around this place are the people that did it years ago – Sir Stanley Matthews, Jimmy Armfield, Stan Mortensen – and I want you to be up there one day and I want you to be remembered, but this is why you're doing it. Just take a minute . . .' I thanked the families for a moment, then I checked with the lads to make sure they understood the tactics and knew what they needed to do, and the players were absolutely on it and ready to go. We got the result we needed that day, too.

It's all about doing what you feel is right at the time – and some of it will be wrong. My mate Phil Brown tried and did what he felt was right at that particular moment in time and it didn't work, but you can only be yourself. I'm glad I diversified at times and some of it worked, some didn't. I tried things at Leicester City, but nothing worked and we got relegated from the Championship.

My mate Tony Pulis got promoted from the Championship the same day I took Leicester down and I totally failed with that club. I talked with the players about family and what staying up would mean ahead of our last game away to Stoke, but we missed a sitter from two yards that would have put us 1–0 up and been enough to save us so we ended up drawing 0–0. That's life, and you have to be what you feel because if you try and be something you're not feeling, the players will smell it. They won't believe you.

As a manager, you're on a journey to find your authentic self, to actually know yourself better than you ever did, so you can have a chance to help someone else in their own life.

10

Centre-forwards: Handle with Care

'Don't feckin' tell me what it's like being a centre-forward, because you haven't had the pressure that I've had to play under.'

Your centre-forwards are your prized racehorses. One of the most important things, when coaching your players, is to do position-specific training, particularly for your thorough-breds – the strikers. If they don't score goals for you and finish all the good work that you do as a team, you're not going to get those points in the bag anytime soon.

I've always felt that you have to treat your No 9s a little bit differently to everyone else, with a combination of some management TLC and the help of a proper finishing coach. Gary Penrice, who I had the pleasure of working with for a number of years, was a proven finisher and could score goals, so Pen, for me, was the ideal coach for my centre-forwards.

During training at Rovers and at most of the clubs I man-aged, as a group we'd all do something together, but I decided to send our centre-forwards over to Pen almost every day to get them doing things one-on-one with him to make them better at their job, before they rejoined the main session. As soon as I started doing this and showing them a bit of TLC to make them feel special and valued, you could see the difference it made to their confidence levels.

I realised that if I was going to actively seek out younger forwards and then try to improve and eventually sell them on – which was a financial lifeline for clubs like Rovers – I needed a coach with a proven goalscoring track record. With my strike rate of about one goal every twelve games when I was a player, that person wasn't me. Why would they bother listening to me? Pen was the best specialist forwards' coach I ever saw. You ask any of the strikers we worked with, and they will tell you the same thing; because of the methods he used, his honesty and his understanding of what it took to be a striker, he helped them all.

Paul Furlong was 36 when I was manager at QPR and he had hit a bad patch and was having trouble hitting a prover-bial barn door with his finishing, so I called Pen, who wasn't on my staff at that time and had moved into scouting.

'Pen, I'm having trouble with Paul Furlong. He keeps missing chances.'

'Whatever you do,' said Pen, 'don't say that to him, Ollie.'

What was I doing wrong? I asked Pen if he'd come down and spend a bit of time with Furs and he was more than happy to do that. He arrived a few days later and I said to Furs, 'This is my mate Gary Penrice, he helped Jason Roberts and a few other strikers we've worked with.'

Furs was open to anything, and Pen said, 'We'll do a bit of a session after training and see what you're good at.'

'Missing,' said Furs with a smile.

'No,' said Pen, 'I've come here to help you and focus on what you can do well.'

'Yeah, I'm good at missing.'

After the main session, Pen headed over to a training pitch with Furs and said, 'OK, you come as well, Ollie – we won't need a keeper. Get a bag of balls and two poles.'

So that's what we did. Pen asked me to put the poles one pace away on the outside of each post. He then said, 'Right, take half the balls on the left and cross them in. Furs, I want you to finish in-between the poles at the side of the goal.'

'What?' said Furs, looking bemused.

'You told me you were good at missing, so show me how good you are at missing. You've got one touch to do it, so let's see how long it takes for you to get it into that gap, because that's not an easy thing to do, is it?'

Furs was just smiling and agreed it wouldn't be easy, but the first cross I put in, he headed it into the gap between the right-hand side of the post and the pole, so he'd done it with his first attempt.

'That's enough, Ollie,' Pen shouted. 'Let's do the other side. You got that one, Furs, one out of one.'

Furs was still giggling. 'Look, I'm deadly serious,' said Pen. 'I asked you what you were good at, you told me missing and that wasn't bad, was it?'

I crossed it from the right, bang – he did it again – straight into the gap between the left post and the pole and Pen shouted, 'Right, that's it.'

Furs looked at me, then looked at Pen and started laughing.

Pen said, 'Look, all I'm saying to you is that maybe your thought process ain't right. If you're as accurate as you just showed you can be, instead, why don't you think "I'm gonna score here"? It's your thought process that's wrong – there's nothing wrong with you. You'll be fine. Change your mindset. You're too good to miss. You will score goals. Keep getting in the right positions and just realign your thinking.'

The transformation was almost immediate. That season he started banging them in for fun, and for the rest of Furs' career, until he hung his boots up, he scored once in every three games – and that was because Pen had showed him how silly his thinking had been and his attitude of 'oh, I will score one day' was making him believe it was alright to miss. Furs later thanked me for getting him help. He'd just hit a mental block and Pen had helped him move past it.

If Pen had helped his thinking, I had to help Furs with his fitness. He never went out and trained fully because of the past injuries he'd had. He'd once ripped some of his thigh off the bone, just by training and running. As a result, he wasn't training hard enough and I told him so.

'Look Furs, you've got to train like you play.'

'No, I can't, boss – I've got to save myself now that I'm getting older.'

Unbelievable. 'No, no, no!' I said. 'You've got to do the opposite! You've got to work harder in training because you're not stretching yourself enough and you'll get injured when you play matches. I can't have you half-training – let's go for it and I'll get you fitter and then you won't get injured. Unless you do it in training, mate, you've got no chance of playing.'

By the end of it, he agreed with me because it's a bit like stretching an elastic band – unless you keep pulling it, pulling it, pulling it, it's never going to get any bigger, is it? So, by under-training, when he went flat out into a game, his body wasn't ready for it.

Ollie's Tip: As a manager you've got to try and make your team feel invincible, however you can; and the personal touches to help them, when things aren't going well, are absolutely paramount to get the best out of everybody.

Pen helped so many strikers when they were in a bad spot.

Jason Roberts was also having a difficult time when he was with us at Bristol Rovers. Jason had come to us via Wolves, Torquay and Bristol City – the latter didn't help his cause much – and he hadn't really got going since signing for us. We knew he had the tools to be our No 9, but he was getting stick from the fans and it was affecting his concentration. Pen told him he had an ego problem and that he shouldn't be listening to what the crowd was saying because it put him off his game. 'I'm gonna have to cure you of that,' he told him.

So Pen and I arranged a shooting session with Jason, plus a goalkeeper. Jason had to ping it in to me, I'd lay it off back into his path and Jason would finish it off. Meanwhile, Pen was having a right go and shouting all sorts of things at him from behind the goal. Jason was fuming. Afterwards Pen said, 'Look, you shouldn't be listening to me, should you? That's the whole point of this, you idiot. You've got to get focused, because you will score goals – at the minute, you can be easily put off. You're more like John McEnroe and I want you to be Bjorn Borg.'

It was incredible what Pen did for him. It took him thirty minutes, and just one session, and in the end, Jason was like a machine. It was all about mindsets, and Pen understood that because he knew what the pressure to score was like.

Gerry Francis had put him up front – which is where he played as a kid – after he'd been playing in midfield, where he was more than capable because he was a wonderful footballer. Gerry said, 'You're a centre-forward and you've got to take on the pressure of scoring goals.'

In fact, Pen and I had a massive row once about scoring goals and he said to me, 'Ollie, you get a pat on the back for running around – and you haven't scored for two years. I'm in a goal drought if I go two games without scoring – that's pressure. You've got the player of the year and gone a whole season without scoring, so don't feckin' tell me what it's like being a centre-forward, because you haven't had the pressure that I've had to play under.'

And he was right. So, if you're going to give your forwards specialist training, you need somebody who understands what they are feeling. It was important they knew – and I knew – that there was somebody they could talk to about it, if they needed to share that burden.

It takes a lot more than just one person to manage a team – you've got to delegate. You can't do it all by yourself, because the players will get fed up with your voice. All you can do is give them the weapons to go out there and fight and win. It ain't about you, it's about you helping them over and over again. And once you've seen someone improve themselves, and do better than they ever thought they could, nothing feels better as a manager.

Centre-forwards are a unique breed. I didn't do the same type of training with defenders, midfielders or wide forwards until I went to Blackpool, where I wanted my wingers to be able to finish as well, so I'd take that session. For wide men it was all about movement, because if you are going to score goals, you've got to be moving before the defenders do and out-manoeuvre them. It was about making that a habit and how do you do that? You practise it every day and you do it so often, you don't realise you're doing it. That was something I brought into my management later on in my career when I had a lot of success, because I made it habit-forming.

Ollie's Tip: If you want to be a football manager and follow my methods, do what I did at the end, not at the start! Make it a habit, make them feel special and make it fun and you'll get results.

As a football manager, you can always find something to learn from other sports. I picked up a lot from Wasps Rugby Club when they were training at QPR's facility and we had to share dressing rooms. I spoke with their coach, Shaun Edwards, who told me that he only brought the players together twice a week, and the rest of the time it was position-specific coaching, weights and fitness training. He said they had a wimps board – where players were named and shamed and the 'over-weighters', as they called them, had to be in at 7 a.m. to check on their diets – and a champions board which gave them targets to get bigger and stronger. It was all quite phenomenal, and I adopted so many of the things they were doing to my management in football. It's amazing what you can get from other sports, and you can always find ways of improving your fitness.

When I was thirty-three and still playing, I met a fitness coach called John Gingal who was a runner and he made me twice as fit as I'd ever been – and with less work! I was already the fittest at my club, but he helped me take three minutes off my best time for running seven miles. He made me do things slightly differently. I remember he looked at my running style and told me my left elbow was going out too far when I ran and said I was wasting energy – he was absolutely incredible.

Management in any sport is all about looking after players properly, caring about them and making them feel loved, wanted and needed. For me, the more support staff you have around you, the better it is because the players can listen to different voices and forge friendships with different coaches who can really help them improve their game. If you look at a tennis player, how many coaches and specialists do they have sitting in their box watching on? To summarise, the best and most successful racehorses are the ones that are fed the right food, trained the right way and cared for by the right people. Do that, and you'll have winners in your stable who will clear any hurdles put in front of them.

11

The Post-Match Glass of Wine

*Sir Alex: 'You'll help me win the title if they
(the opposition) turn up and think they'll beat you,
because you'll beat a lot of teams playing like that.'*

You hear some managers say it, don't you? 'I'm going to have a nice glass of wine with such and such,' in their post-match interview but it's a bit of a myth in all honesty.

Not every manager does that, and if you've got a long journey home and you've lost, it's a case of cheers, bye, and you're gone because you don't really want to keep your team waiting on the bus while you indulge yourself. If you've won, sometimes it looks smug if you go into the other manager's office and you don't always get on with the other person anyway.

You've also got your post-match press conferences that don't line up sometimes, so it is a bit of a myth, but that's not to say it doesn't happen with some of the more senior managers and I have partaken in that ritual on the odd occasion myself.

I remember taking my Bristol Rovers side to take on Sam Allardyce's Notts County and my lads were fantastic on the day, and I think we beat them 3–0. After the final whistle, Sam said, 'I think you'd better have a glass of wine with me, young man.'

'Oh brilliant, thanks Sam,' I said, 'but I don't really drink wine.'

'Well that's all I've got so you'd better have a glass – I'm off after this.' I asked what he meant, and he told me he was off to Bolton Wanderers after that game and that was his last match in charge. He'd jumped from a team struggling in the third division, to a mid-table Championship side and I'd just beaten his side 3–0. I wondered, 'How's that work then? How's he got that job and I've got one like this?' And that stayed in my mind. I accepted it was down to experience and of course, what Sam did at Bolton was completely off the charts. Sam had a massive sense of confidence in what he was doing and how he was doing it and that was what I took away with me, because if my team could beat his team like that and he's gone on to bigger things, I needed to feel like he felt because I was still quite young at the time.

Ollie's Tip: You see managers who know where they are and what they're doing and are comfortable in their own skin, so you can get an awful lot out of a post-match glass of wine with them, because of their body language after the game.

I never met Bill Shankly or Brian Clough, but they were managers I looked up to and I used to wonder what made them tick. I've read about them and the things they did and the way they were, but imagine sharing a glass of wine with them? Just think about what you might learn. Incredible.

When I got promoted with Blackpool, that occasional post-match glass of wine became much more important, and I actually looked forward to it. In our first game, we were away to Roberto Martinez's Wigan and beat them 4–0, so we were top of the Premier League for a couple of hours. Roberto was very courteous, really nice, really confident, and complimentary, even though we hadn't deserved to win 4–0. I enjoyed his company and I'm delighted he went on to be so successful.

Next up, we had Arsenal away. In that game, we had the first chance on nine minutes – a back-post header from Gary Taylor-Fletcher and he should have scored, but he headed it wide, which is unlike Fletch, but we were still creating. Two minutes later, they get a chance and Theo Walcott scores. We have a chance and miss. They have a chance and they're 1–0 up. One chance, one goal.

Then we get another opportunity through Keith Southern – not as clearcut, but a chance all the same – and he doesn't score. We're still losing and when Ian Evatt then makes a tackle – I believe just outside the box – the ref points to the spot and sends him off. Arshavin scores, it's 2–0 and we still have sixty minutes or so to play. Oh my God. We're two down, a man down, at the Emirates with ages to play. Everything I'd taught my lads about how Arsenal play and what we needed to do went to dust and we lost 6–0 – and we were lucky it was just six, because it was a living, breathing nightmare.

Now for that glass of wine. I went in to see Arsène afterwards and it was total ruination, really, because I'd wanted him to see how we played and how well we could play at that level and I'd been anticipating a long chat with him, but he was in there talking French with someone. He said a polite 'hello' and indicated he'd be a couple of minutes, so I got my glass of wine in a beautiful crystal glass that weighed a tonne, and was probably sitting there for another ten minutes before he came over and asked me a question that I couldn't answer.

'Let me ask you, what will you do when your team can't dominate the ball like it did last year? What will you do?'

I paused and said, 'Probably lose 6–0.'

And he laughed, before saying, 'No, you need to find an answer. In this division, can you keep the ball against the teams who have been here for years? You have to ask yourself, and you have to have an answer. The next time I see you, try and have an answer.'

I thanked him and went on my way, but I was thinking, 'Oh my God! What on earth? I can't change, I can't do this.'

I couldn't change my philosophy with that team, so I carried on doing what we did the whole season and by the halfway point, we had twenty-eight points, so I thought, actually, I can do it. We can do this. But in the second half of the season, we only got eleven points and we got relegated. I then looked back at what we were doing, and I realised that other teams analysed what we did and by halfway through the season, they understood how we played and nullified it, and I didn't change it.

I looked at what I should have changed, ticked that box, and realised what I should have done. It was too late, but I believe if I'd understood sooner, we'd have stayed up.

The answer? My full-backs, when we were attacking down the opposite side, instead of them both being wide and staying high, I should have tucked the opposite one in and then I'd have had two centre-halves, a sitting midfielder and my right-back in a square. So, anything that was headed out by the other team, we could have got to it first and used it to our advantage, but there were gaps in our formation and our opponents knew if they got through it, and they hit us on the counter behind my opposite full-back, they were in. Now if I'd have brought the left-back in instead of leaving him out wide, I think it would have prevented a lot of problems and won us a few more points.

So, I learned that, but I still hadn't learned how to answer Arsène's question. I was thinking, 'That year's gone by, we've been relegated, and I won't see him again', and I was out of there. I didn't learn how to answer his question until I went to Crystal Palace and the Palace players didn't want to play the same way that I did – they didn't want to have the ball. They didn't want to dominate. What they'd been taught was different to my style, even though the way that they did it was excellent in its own right.

I needed to adapt my own plans because the players weren't comfortable changing and so, in order to get us over the line, I sat down with the analysis guys and they explained what the lads were good at and why. They told me they studied the passing lanes of the opposition and in the run-up to playing them, the sessions were based on blocking those passing lanes by getting bodies in those channels. In the actual game, we would soak up pressure in the grid on the edge of the eighteen-yard box and target three specific areas across the pitch to clear the ball into and then we'd counter-attack.

And it was then I realised that this was what Arsène had been talking about when he'd said, 'when you haven't got the ball, what do you do?' If I'd done that at Blackpool against certain teams who overplayed, everything would have been different. It was like, 'Oh dearie me, how do I do it? Here we go, that's what I do,' and I thought, next time I see him, I'll bloody well tell him.

So, we got Palace up to the Premier League and the next time I bumped into Mr Wenger, I said, 'You asked me a question two years ago, I don't know if you remember? About my Blackpool team . . . you beat us 6–0?'

He nodded, recalling the chat, and said, 'I remember the question – what will you do when you can't dominate the ball?'

'We will block your passing lanes, and we will counterattack against you,' I said.

He smiled and said, 'Well done, young man, well done,' and shook my hand and gave me a hug.

Wow. I wish he'd told me the answer after that 6–0 defeat. I might have kept us up. But it's magical and you have to earn that right. Knowledge is everything and if I could go back, I'd have probably had an older manager alongside me, but I don't know if I was confident enough to do that – what would that look like? Tony Pulis had Gerry Francis alongside him for a while and you need that knowledge; and what if I could have had someone alongside me who had been there, seen that and done it – a mentor, maybe? But I didn't, for whatever reason.

I almost had a glass of wine with Nuno Espírito Santos once and told him I loved the way his team played and we became great friends in that one meeting, because I was in awe of what he was doing at Wolves: to come in, change it totally and play with three at the back and do it the way he did and have seven players attacking the opposition. I said, 'Can we find a weakness?' But we couldn't, and I told him that before the game in my little office at QPR. I said, 'I can't find a weakness in your team.' We managed to win the game, but we didn't deserve to, and he was so grateful for the words I'd said to him. We didn't have wine because he didn't have time, but we had a quick coffee.

And no story of post-match glasses of wine would be complete without the king of them all, Sir Alex Ferguson. My Blackpool side lost twice against his United side in the Premier League with an aggregate of 7–4, which ain't bad! We lost 3–2 at our place and had been 2–1 up but lost 4–2 at Old Trafford. He'd made telling substitutions, and I couldn't do that because my squad wasn't big enough and all the best lads started.

At our place, I got the best crystal glass and the best bottle of wine that we had from upstairs – being the Oystons, there wasn't much choice – and he was smiling and laughing because he'd won. We'd been leading 2–0 at half-time, he'd taken off Wayne Rooney and brought on Berbatov and took off another and brought on Ryan Giggs and they scored three goals in the last twenty minutes.

Sir Alex complimented me about the movement of our front lads and said he didn't know what we were doing with them, but it was fantastic and well done and keep it going.

I'd told my forwards to keep moving and never stand still and we practised automatic movements where one covered the area the other had been in, and they kept rotating that movement. It took a while to get right, but by the time we got to the Premier League, we were doing it brilliantly. Sir Alex had noticed it, mentioned it, and said, 'You'll help me win the title if they (the opposition) turn up and think they'll beat you, because you'll beat a lot of teams playing like that.'

We beat Liverpool twice that season and for the game at Bloomfield Road, Kenny Dalglish was in charge, and I think he must have tried to go into my office, but I was already upstairs with Karl who was cock-a-hoop. Kenny came up and I almost melted! He was always a hero of mine, but he made the effort to come up and say how well he thought my players had done and was so complimentary about the way we'd played – and particularly Charlie Adam, who he thought was fantastic. Karl was actually quite nice to him – because it was Kenny Dalglish – and he was just a wonderful man.

So those after-match glasses of wine can be humiliating if you've just been smashed, but enlightening and everything else in-between. The idea is you're having time with other professionals who do what you do for a living and then sharing ideas, but it doesn't really happen – I wish it did, but it doesn't. Really, you need to get a few managers together, sit down and share ideas, and that would be one hell of a way to come up with new things – because that's what the best are doing at the moment, and I'm talking about Pep Guardiola and Jürgen Klopp in particular.

Their teams dominate you and then they strangle you. Then they dominate you again, strangle you some more and opposition managers must be thinking, 'Christ, this is terrible – it's horrific, what's going on?' And if you don't know how they do it, and you can't do it back to them, maybe just sit on the edge of your own box and try and counter-attack. Every now and then you might win against them doing that, but most of the time they're just going to dominate you and it's a case of how many are you going to concede.

Improving players

As a player, I'd watch footballers I admired and wonder what made them tick. Gerry Francis was the first manager I played under to tell me how I could become a better player. The minute I met Gerry, I thought 'Oh my God' because he was my inspiration and the man who made me want to be a manager.

He'd tell me what I got wrong, but he wouldn't totally blame me. He would blame the other person next to me who should have half-marked my man as well as marking his own man, because my man might get the ball. You never mark your opposition player 100 per cent if he hasn't got the ball – you only start to mark him 100 per cent as the ball is on its way to him. And then everybody else marks a man and a half – they've got their man, but they've got half yours as well. So, Gerry would teach us to look for the three mistakes for every goal and it was like, hallelujah – because all I wanted to do was to get better, but I didn't know how to because previously when things hadn't gone well, I'd just been told – by almost everybody – 'you had a bad game today'. Yeah, but why?' Gerry would say, 'You had a bad game today because you need to turn your shoulder a quarter-turn away, because otherwise you can't see him in your peripheral vision. If you turn that quarter more, you'll have a bigger picture and you'll be a better player.'

12

Contract Negotiations

'I don't care . . . Have his agent look at the league table and then tell him to fuck off.'

As a manager, you don't usually get that involved in contract negotiations – that's down to the chairman or chief executive – but in the earlier part of my career I would occasionally take part, especially if I was trying to convince someone to join or extend their deal.

The player's agent always wants that bit extra and for you to throw in this or that for their client, and you expect that, but sometimes I needed to think outside the box in order to try and get a signature over the line.

Marcus Stewart at Bristol Rovers was a case in point. 'Stewie' was out of contract and there was a ruling that said he could sign for a club abroad for free, meaning Rovers wouldn't get a penny for a striker that had done really well for us and was still only twenty-four. He was a Bristol lad, but determined to move on, so I had a plan in my head to try and at least keep his registration so we could get a fee if he did move on.

Phil Purnell – Purce – who I'd played alongside at Rovers was his agent, so I asked them both to come in to talk about the current status quo.

In a meeting in my office, I told Stewie what I thought about everything and that I wanted him to stay, but he said, 'No, I want to go, Ol. Rovers haven't been fair to me, the contract offer wasn't good enough, so I don't want to stay here anymore.'

I asked who he was going to sign for and he said that was none of my business at the minute and that he just wanted to go. I told him I thought he was good enough to play at a higher level, so I picked the phone up and called Kevin Keegan at Newcastle United and said, 'I heard you might be interested in Marcus Stewart, and I've got him here with me now.'

'I am interested,' said Keegan, 'but I've heard some rumours about him.'

I knew what the rumours were about. Stewie used to occasionally go out on a Saturday night with his old school mates who thought it was funny to get him drunk every now and then.

'Well, Kev, you can speak to him now if you like?'

I handed the phone to Stewie and Keegan said to him, 'Ollie says you're a great lad, so if you play well for the next few weeks, I might be interested in signing you.'

I took the phone back off Stewie, thanked Keegan and hung up.

'I'm still not signing,' insisted Stewie.

'What, even after that phone call? I've got to sell you.'

Purce asked what I meant, and I said, 'The club's going to go bust if we don't sell him.'

'Ollie, unless you can improve anything,' said Purce, 'he ain't going to stay and he probably won't stay anyway.'

I told him to leave it with me and they both left. I got straight on the phone to our chairman, Geoff Dunford, but he just said he wasn't going to give Stewie anything other than the deal he'd offered.

'He's not going to sign then,' I said.

'I don't want him to sign,' Geoff replied, 'but I don't want him going on a free, so if you can get proof that he's turned down a contract offer, we keep his registration and we still get paid for him.'

We needed to improve Stewie's offer, otherwise legally he could sign for a club overseas and we'd get nothing because the deal he'd been offered was on the same terms he was already on.

I told Geoff to leave it with me and so I decided to improve the contract offer myself! I knew what Stewie wanted – a brand new Toyota MR2, which cost a fair bit of money. So, I spoke with Graham Bowen, our commercial manager and asked if he could get an MR2. If we could get somebody to buy it for us, I told him that I would pay them back once we'd sold Stewie.

He asked me to explain it better, so I said, 'I want a Rovers fan to buy Stewie an MR2 – sponsor him, in effect – and we'll pay the garage back out of the transfer fee we get for him. I need that car.'

Graham called up a local petrolhead who owned a garage and did a lot for the club and called me back an hour or so later to say, 'Ollie, I've managed to do it. This guy will pay the first two or three months' finance and if we sell Stewie, we'll pay the garage off and he'll keep the car for himself, but he won't take a penny until Stewie's gone.'

I said, 'Brilliant! Can we get him to deliver to the training ground with a big bow tied around it?'

Then I spoke to the chairman and said, 'Surely the price of an MR2 isn't going to kill you if we get a good fee for him? And he's going to turn it down anyway. I've improved the contract and got somebody else to pay for it, so all you've got to do is pay for the car if he signs the contract, which he ain't gonna do, is he? So, by the end of the day we'll have sent the car back because he will do what you want and turn down the offer.'

'Are you suggesting that it won't cost me any money and we can still get him to sign the papers?'

'Exactly! He's not going to accept the contract offer. You could put a feckin' Rolls-Royce in there and he wouldn't sign it, would he?'

'OK, go on then . . .'

If Stewie did accept the new deal and the car, I'd already worked out how we could pay for it, plus I'd get to keep a top striker for a bit longer, so it was a foolproof plan.

The car was delivered as requested and I called Purce and Stewie back in and the MR2 was parked outside the training ground when they arrived. I'd amended the contract to have the MR2 included in it as a signing-on incentive and said, 'That's your car, Stewie. If you sign the new contract I've sorted, when you leave here, that car is yours. Or you can turn it down now, but you've got to do it in writing.'

He said he still wanted to go, and I said, 'Are you sure you don't want that car? You told me Rovers never get you anything, but I appreciate you and I've got you this.'

'Stewie, do you understand what Ollie is saying?' said Purce.

'Look,' said Stewie, 'I need to leave.'

'You can have the car,' said Purce, 'because Ollie is still going to sell you.'

'I'm sorry, I've got to go. I don't believe that contract is right.'

He actually signed the document confirming he'd turned down a better, improved offer and it turned out he was signing for Huddersfield Town who would pay us £1.2 million because we had his registration. Geoff Dunford drove to the training ground and gave me a massive hug because he could have gone overseas for free.

That's the only time I've ever got that actively involved in a contract deal and we came out of it rather well, I think. I was gutted to lose him, because I wanted to keep him for a bit longer, but the money we received enabled us to get Jamie Cureton, Bobby Zamora and Barry Hayles as well as keeping the club afloat. A good bit of business, even if I do say so myself.

Stewie went on to have a great career and scored goals for Huddersfield, Ipswich and Sunderland as I knew he would. Just before this book went to press, I learned he had been diagnosed with motor neurone disease. I've no doubt he will tackle that with the same determination he tackles everything else. He is a marvellous lad.

Ollie's Tip: Sometimes you have to be a bit slippery when you're negotiating a contract, and sometimes you have to include clauses that can actually come back and bite the person that insisted on their inclusion in the first place.

Another case in point was Charlie Adam. I managed to get Charlie on loan from Rangers, but he'd been loaned around for the past five years, and I had a chance to sign him permanently. Matt Williams was our chief executive at Blackpool in everything but name and he had great contacts all around the country.

Matt told me we had an opportunity to get Charlie and that the chairman Karl Oyston was aware of it. He said, 'Preston are really interested, but we can't let him go there, can we?'

We sat down with Karl and explained the situation. 'We can't afford what Rangers are asking,' he said. 'Preston have more money than us, so we're just going to have to let him go. Find me another one.'

Karl believed that you should always be able to walk away from a deal if you're not happy. In his mind, you had to be able to say, 'Nah, that's not right for us – we have somebody else lined up, so we'll go and sign him instead.' He said you should never go into a deal wanting to sign just one person and you should always have five targets. He said I should never, ever present him with just the one.

It all made sense and I had no problem with that, but I said, 'Yeah, but there's only one Charlie Adam. I believe in him, our lads believe in him and if he goes anywhere, it should be to us.'

Karl said it was OK saying that, but he was only going to pay a certain amount.

Matt was very persuasive and had worked with Karl long before I arrived and he said, 'Karl, you know how good

Charlie is. The fans will go mental, it will put a few extra people on your gate if we get him permanently and he's worth twice his money and you know that. I don't think Preston have any money – it's all smoke and mirrors. I think we can get him for £500,000 so why don't we do the right thing and offer that for him? They've asked for a million, but I think that will get him and you can add a sell-on because you'll make money on him – he's getting better all the time.'

We offered £500,000 and Rangers accepted – but Karl really only wanted to pay £350,000! Matt came back and said they'd told him to fuck off, but as it was, in the end we did the deal for £500,000 and Karl didn't stop moaning for about three months. To get the deal over the line, we had to put a clause in Charlie's contract that if a top-six Premier League club came in for him, we would talk to them and try and negotiate a deal for him to go.

I said to Charlie that I would give him my word that if he could get better than us before we could grow – like I believed we would – then I couldn't do much more for him, and if we got a call from a team in the top six, we'd do a deal. Charlie was happy with the agreement, we got the contract signed and it was happy days.

He did so well for us and scored nineteen goals from mid-field on our way to promotion to the Premier League. All of a sudden, we're in the top flight and he's playing fantastically well – everyone was talking about Charlie Adam – so when it gets to January, Charlie comes in to see me and brings his agent Kenny Moyes with him. Kenny says, 'Charlie wants to leave. Tell him yourself, Charlie.'

Charlie said, 'I want to go, gaffer. Liverpool want me.'

Kenny confirmed Liverpool had been in touch, so I said that I'd put it to Karl and see what he said.

Liverpool did call me with an official approach shortly after, and I told them they needed to speak to Karl and Matt because I didn't deal with any of that.

I spoke with Matt and said we had a problem, but he said why didn't we make this an opportunity to invest in the team because we'd probably get £5 million or more for Charlie – he's going to go one day anyway. With that money, I'd be able to give two new contracts to David Vaughan and DJ Campbell and make Jason Puncheon's loan permanent. I could also probably bring someone else in, all for losing one player. That's four players secured, plus I'd have kept my word and Charlie had his dream move.

If anyone ever wants to leave your club, you have to get them gone.

Liverpool rang Karl, and to my horror, he said, 'Not interested in talking to you. He's not for sale.'

I called Matt and he said, 'Ollie, you'll have to come up and see him. He's in one of those moods.'

When Karl was in 'one of those moods', he was stubborn as hell and it was pretty much 'no, no, no, no,' to everything.

I got to the ground and went to see Karl, knocked on his door and he shouted, 'If you're going to ask for Charlie Adam to leave, you're not coming in.'

Eventually, he buzzed me in, and I sat down and said, 'What are you doing, then?'

He asked if I'd seen Charlie's contract and I said I had.

'It says top-six club, right?' he said. I agreed it did. 'Well, where are they in the league? Seventh. So, how dare they try to activate that clause when they're not in the top six.'

'Karl, it's Liverpool.'

'I don't care,' he replied. 'Have his agent look at the league table and then tell him to fuck off.'

He asked if I'd spoken to Matt, and I said I had. Then he said, 'How can selling our best player make us a better team? I don't agree with you, and I don't have to sell him, so I'm not.'

Karl wouldn't budge and just said, 'Seventh, not sixth.'

Charlie then turned up with his agent because it was the last day of the January transfer window. Karl said, 'I'll let Charlie in, but his agent can fuck right off.'

He eventually relented because Kenny Moyes had helped us with Seamus Coleman, but I knew he'd stick to his guns no matter what. And that meant sticking to the letter of the law and following the exact wording of any agreement.

He told Charlie, 'I wrote that in there and I still mean it now. Words are important and I wrote them correctly, so what does it say in your contract? I don't want to sell you to Liverpool, and I don't have to sell you to Liverpool. Liverpool are not in the top six and you're not for sale. You can put a transfer request in and do what you like, but I am not going to sell you. That's it.'

Kenny said Liverpool would pay £6 million and Karl said, 'I don't need £6 million. Charlie helped me get £150 million last year – why do I want to sell my best player? Just go away and read the contract you were happy to sign and stop moaning. Now fuck off. End of story.'

I asked Charlie if anyone in the top six wanted to sign him and Kenny said that Spurs were interested – but that Charlie wanted to join Liverpool. I said there was nothing I could do there, but if a top six club came in, maybe he'd then consider Liverpool's offer because he could legally move on anyway, but technically, Karl was just confirming what was already written in stone.

Kenny rang Harry Redknapp and he called me and asked how good was Charlie. I said brilliant, but he said he wasn't sure if they had any money. I went to see Karl and said Spurs might be interested and he said, 'Are you trying to sell my best player? I'm not interested, and I've had enough because I want to stay in the league and Charlie can help us do that.'

I felt like I was breaking my promise to Charlie and tried one more time, saying that we'd make £5.5 million if we sold him, but he just said, 'That's what you do – I just have to make the right decisions for Blackpool Football Club and I like Charlie and I don't want him to go anywhere, so you'll have to motivate him after I've demotivated him.'

But I don't believe I ever managed to do that. In the first half of the season, we got twenty-eight points – in the second half, we got eleven and went down by one point. Had Charlie not had his head turned, would it have made a difference? I think so. Had we sold him and strengthened the team and tied up others on longer contracts, would that have made a difference? I think it would – but if my auntie had bollocks, she'd be my uncle. All ifs, buts and maybes and we'll never know what would have happened.

As things panned out, after we were relegated Charlie signed for Liverpool anyway for £6 million. In a strange way, the overall outcome of this transfer saga was that Karl made me manage better than ever before, because I could see his point about sticking to the exact terms of a contract. We also got Tom Ince coming the other way for £250,000 after Paul Ince called me and asked if I could get his son away from Liverpool. He wanted me to get him playing the way we played at Blackpool and get him going again. What a compliment that was. I asked Pen and he said that we couldn't lose, it was like getting a racehorse out of a fantastic stable and we were getting Tom for practically nothing. He was worth taking a gamble on – and what a player he turned out to be for us.

13

Press Conferences and the Media

'I thought his bum cheeks looked very pert. If anybody's offended by that, they ought to go and see the doctor.'

One of the biggest areas of football management is learning to deal and work with the media.

Maybe it's the biggest challenge of them all. It's something you learn about as you become a more experienced manager – how to deal with it, how to control it and yourself when you're conducting an interview or a press conference, and how important it is to get everything right. It's all about the image you're projecting and it's a delicate balancing act on a tightrope that you can fall off at any point, so it's vital you get the media on your side – and that's not an easy skill to have.

You have to talk to the media thirty minutes after a game and if your team hasn't played well, you will probably get a question you don't like, but there's no use being like a porcupine and getting all your quills up ready to go. Even if you can be a prickly bastard!

I've always said it like it is and a lot of the media seem to like that – and the supporters as well – but I'm not saying that's always the best way to be. I'm saying that's the only way I could be. I've adapted and developed over the years to be an awful lot better than I once was.

At Bristol Rovers, it was my Achilles heel because any question I was asked, I had my back up ready to have a fight. I'd gone from being a player straight into management and I hadn't had time to think. It was my club, so I was so emotionally invested anyway and when I was asked a question that I didn't like, I would fire back with 'Why'd you ask me that?' I was always ready for a scrap.

When I was Rovers manager, there was one reporter working for the local paper who was quite openly a Bristol City fan, and he must have thought I hated him. He wrote a match report after we'd played Bristol City and drawn 0–0 and claimed that if Bristol City had my two strikers – who, in that game, were rubbish, by the way – then City would be a team Bristol could be proud of. Boom! So, Rovers couldn't be that team? That ignited my blue touch paper just a bit, so I invited him to the training ground. He didn't know why, but I knew – for once, I was going to make someone front up to what they'd written and experience what the reaction was like.

It's all well and good tapping away on your laptop, but would you write the same crap if you actually had to say it to the players in question? So, when he arrived, I went to meet him and I said, 'You are going to apologise to my team, you bastard.' I took him into a room where all my players were sat down. Then I had the two centre-halves stand up. I said, 'Right, now tell these two – who you only gave five out of ten each – just how well you think they played, you asshole.'

He'd ask me something after a game and I'd literally want to kill him because of his allegiance to Bristol City. In all honesty, looking back now I realise it wasn't really fair at all on him and I got that wrong, but the point is, if you don't agree with what is being said, make sure you let it be known.

For the record, that reporter left sports journalism and started writing about other stuff, but we are good friends now and thankfully, we can look back at it and smile. I think.

The other thing that football managers have to face on a regular basis is the ubiquitous press conference. When you're at a lower league club, press conferences don't hold a great deal of interest for journalists other than maybe the local paper and one or two others. At Bristol Rovers, I'd have perhaps three or four at the pre-game presser and it wasn't until I managed in the Premier League that I realised how big and important they were.

Every week, you'd find a whole room packed with journos from everywhere and I soon discovered that I really liked doing them. To begin with, when I was at Blackpool the team were doing well and I suppose the journalists who attended our press conferences would go off-piste about what I thought about this and that, looking for an amusing headline that I was usually happy to supply. I looked forward to the Thursday presser where I enjoyed giving my opinion on anything and everything.

Ollie's Tip: My advice for any manager speaking to journalists would be that you have to be your authentic self in everything you say and do. If you don't, you're not living right because you can't hold back. Say what you feel and think.

The only problem is, I got into some terrible trouble by telling the truth – and it cost me a fortune in the end!

I was asked how I felt about players lifting their shirts when they score and whether they should be booked or not and I said, 'If there are any ladies watching they might like to see a man rip off his shirt and show the old washboard stomach.' And I meant it.

In 2006, Joey Barton dropped his shorts after Man City scored a late equaliser away to Everton, probably because of the stick the home crowd had been giving him, and I was asked what I thought about it. I didn't agree with the abuse that Joey got that day. The kid was having enough problems at the time and I couldn't believe the scathing reaction from the Everton fans when all he'd done was go over to give a disabled kid his shirt.

All he did was show his ass to those who were giving him plenty and I don't think anybody should really be offended by something like that. For the FA to try and then charge him with some kind of offence was ridiculous – I thought that at the time, and I still think the same way now.

My response was, 'It was a bit cheeky, wasn't it? But I don't think it was that bad. It would have been worse if he'd turned round and dropped the front of his shorts instead. I don't think there's anything wrong with a couple of butt cheeks, personally. I think he's a funny lad and he was having a joke. I don't think he meant to offend anybody. If anybody's offended by seeing a backside, get real.

'Maybe they're just jealous that he's got a real nice tight one, with no cellulite or anything. I thought his bum cheeks looked very pert. If anybody's offended by that they ought to go and see the doctor.'

That week in training, instead of the infamous yellow jersey, I had two pairs of Joey Barton shorts made with a cut-out for each bum cheek and then one of those comedy asses from the joke shop – one black, one white – and the worst trainers of the day had to wear them and run around as though their ass was hanging out.

But what you quickly realise is that whatever you say, there's no limit to how far it might go and how much they might twist it. Once it's out there, it's out there for good and you have to be really, really careful.

Another time, I said that with the size of your club and depending on what you're doing, you have to cut your suit accordingly. That's a saying I've heard many, many times but they changed one word and it made me sound like an absolute asshole. I think they wrote that I'd said 'cut your soup accordingly' or something along those lines. Whether the journo was lazy or mischievous, I'll never know, but there's a book out there with my quotes, *The Tao of Ian Holloway*, which I didn't endorse – and that quote is in it. If you read it, I'd just add an advisory. I didn't necessarily say it! I have enough problems controlling what I say myself without somebody adding things I didn't say!

To think that I've had that quote thrown back at me so many times, but I didn't even say it in the first place. What a load of bollocks that is.

When I'm enjoying myself, I'm not sure I am careful with my words, but when it's twisted back against you, that's when it goes wrong. I've used phrases, stories and expressions to galvanise my players into thinking the way that I want them to, and I don't believe there is anything wrong with that so long as you get your point across.

My press conferences at Crystal Palace proved to be particularly tough for some reason. It began with endless questions about Wilfried Zaha and went on and on from game to game. Wilfried is a fantastic player, don't get me wrong, but there was a hell of a lot more going on at Palace at the time. In the end, it started to needle me because the whole ethos we were trying to create was about being a team and everyone being equally important. A lot of players were doing really well, but nobody asked me about them, so I started getting a bit funny with a few of the journalists – never a wise thing.

I said to one, 'Wilfried is a massive part of what we are doing, but do you realise this team that we've got has more than one player? Why don't you ask me about Mile Jedinak who is one of the finest leaders I've ever worked with, on the pitch and off the pitch? Why don't you ask me about Yannick Bolasie on the other wing? Why don't you ask me about Glenn Murray, who's scored thirty goals already this season, or Damien Delaney and his story or how he's doing this season? Or Julian Speroni and some of the things he's doing in goal? There's more to Crystal Palace than Wilfried Zaha. Why is it always Wilf? Why always the same fella? Why? I don't get it. Are you just being lazy?'

And boy, oh boy – they didn't like that.

The thing was, Wilf was attracting a lot of interest because his agent's contract was halfway through the final year, so he was trying to get him a move to get one final pay-out on him, but it was starting to put Wilf off his game. I needed him to play well, so I tried to manipulate the press in order to take some of the pressure off his shoulders.

In the end, I went to see our chairman about how difficult the press conferences were becoming and wondered if there was any way we could resolve Wilf's problem. He asked what the problem was, and I said, 'His agent's trying to get him a move and you know his agent very well – he's your mate! So, why don't we sell him and try and loan him back? The speculation is getting worse and it's not going to stop and it's ruining him.'

He asked what I meant, so I said, 'If we sold him with the agreement of loaning him back for the rest of the season, whether we go up or not, he's going to be motivated – or give him a new deal.'

He said he tried to offer him a new deal, but he didn't want to sign it, so I said we should try my idea and see where that took us. The chairman said that nobody had enquired about him. 'OK,' I said, 'why don't I get in touch with Man United and tell them Arsenal have been sniffing around for him – I'm sure Sir Alex could make him one hell of a player.'

So, I did. I called Sir Alex and said that Wilf was a fantastic footballer and he said, 'Funnily enough, my son has just told me the same thing' – we'd played Peterborough a few weeks before and Wilf had been outstanding, scoring a last-minute winner after we cleared a corner, and he broke forward beating God knows how many players. He asked me what I was thinking, and I said that he was totally unsettled because of his agent and Sir Alex said he thought it might be doable.

So, I spoke to the chairman, spoke to Wilf, and arranged for him to go up to Manchester to meet Sir Alex and Bobby Charlton and have a chat about Manchester United. And that's what happened – Wilf went up there, we agreed a fee and he was loaned back to us. That resolved a problem that had surfaced all because of the questioning at a press conference.

And isn't it funny? Wilf scored twice in the Championship play-off semi-final and won us the penalty in the final where Kevin Phillips scored the winner to take us up to the Premier League. And all that without our thirty-one-goal leading scorer Glenn Murray. So I'm sorry, but I'm claiming that big time!

When I started to be a bit different at press conferences, I was trying to correct just how wrong I'd got it at Bristol Rovers.

Being in the top division was a world away from what I'd been used to, so when there were press conferences, it was like, 'What? How many?'

And in London, there were so many papers around that all had opinions – some of them free that you pick up on buses and trains – so, everything is out there, all the time. It was huge, and I decided I wanted to embrace it and just be myself. So that was the beginning of me being me at press conferences.

Food for thought: Do I regret some of the things I said? Yes, but mostly because it wasn't taken the way I meant it to be, like the 'let's have coffee' quote. I opened up about how I am with my players to the media because I knew I had to be my authentic self, so that's the time that everything really changed.

I wasn't aggressive with them, I felt I could answer questions openly and honestly and I felt it really helped me at QPR, because the troubles we ended up in during my tenancy were quite incredible. We were the first big club to go into administration – and nobody really knew what that meant in football until the administrators came in. I had seven players left at the end of that season when we went down, plus long-term cruciate ligament injuries to Richard Langley and Clarke Carlisle – two of my best players – and no goalie. And no staff. So, all the things that I started saying at press conferences happened after we'd been through that.

There was talk we'd have to merge with Wimbledon, lose Loftus Road and share their ground and I said, 'Are you kidding? I'm not losing our cave.' I felt like a caveman and that's where it all started, and as I say, I don't regret it – apart from if anyone thinks I was chasing girls and asking them into a taxi for a coffee, because I've never done that. That quote came when I was QPR boss and I'd been trying to get across that sometimes the end result is all that matters.

I said, 'To put it in gentleman's terms if you've been out for a night and you're looking for a young lady and you pull one, some weeks they're good looking and some weeks they're not the best. Our performance today would have been not the best-looking bird but at least we got her in the taxi. She wasn't the best-looking lady we ended up taking home, but she was very pleasant and very nice, so thanks very much, let's have a coffee.'

OK, I didn't get that one right. But I'd met my wife at school, and I was likening it to being at a school disco and leaving before the lights came up, because when they did and everyone could see me, they'd have buggered off anyway. It was another one of my unusual ways of explaining to the lads that it was about getting some wins – even if you win ugly.

Player protection

At QPR I was trying to protect one of my players – one of my best-paid players – who was having terrible trouble off the field. But because he'd gone missing, and I hadn't seen him for some time, I was like 'Where is he? What's he doing?' and I just knew that I couldn't say any of that to the press.

I couldn't talk about that when I wanted to be really open – it wouldn't have been right – so I had to then answer twenty questions about where he was and so I said, 'Now will you ask me about the bloody game?' It had been a fantastic result and we'd beaten Bury 3–0, but it was a terrible performance in the second half because we almost threw it away. They should have scored and that performance wasn't good enough, and I didn't want my players thinking that had been OK. Then it all got a bit weird with me saying that the performance had not been 'good-looking' and sometimes it was OK 'to win ugly', but it all came from the tension and pressure of trying to protect Clarke Carlisle. I was trying to deflect everything away from what was actually happening because I knew it was very serious.

It was the first time I ever experienced trying to help someone who was really personally deep in something that he wasn't able to deal with and which he had to admit to me before I could get him some help.

So, I read up on it all but the press was very difficult to deal with, because I think some of them knew and they didn't want to say. They wanted to come and meet me to discuss it because they don't miss much, do they? But as a manager and as a football club, you have a duty of care that goes all the way back to the basics of your player being safe and secure in his life with his family, and if one of them needs anything, then I am there to help in any way possible. I am there to relieve that pressure from him so he can play with a free mind, because no one in the world plays their best if they're carrying trouble.

Clarke had to go missing for twenty-eight days for me to be able to get him some help at a rehab clinic and I said to my chairman we should pay for that and he asked, 'And keep paying him?' I said yes, we have a duty of care to get him mentally and physically right, so we need to do it and, in the end, they supported me by doing it.

The PFA should look after that side of things, but in this instance the mental health charity Sporting Chance were there to help Clarke. I told my lads what was happening and said, 'If this was you, I would be doing the same thing, so we keep that amongst us, and I don't want to hang it out there about what he is struggling with.' Eventually, Clarke shared his problems with people which is a testament to the man.

Ollie's Tip: The minute you sign a player, he is yours and you have to look after him, and that should go all the way down to whatever issues they have. As manager of a player in a tough situation, I always asked myself, 'What would I do if it was my boy? What would I do?' Luckily, I had children, so I understood that I had to look after this guy, and with any scenario that comes up, I always start with that same question.

14

Referees: How (and how not) to Deal With Them

'Plymouth: Managed by Ian Holloway – loud-mouthed, argumentative, team has no discipline. Be aware!'

To say I have a chequered past with match officials is something of an understatement. I've been sent off, fined and banned more times than I can remember and the thing I finally realised in the end was, I got it completely wrong.

My favourite referee during my playing days was Paul Durkin because he was the first official that I ever heard swearing on a pitch. I remember questioning a decision of his and he went, 'Fuck off, that wasn't a foul!' It was quite shocking at the time, I don't mind admitting. He'd be like, 'Stop your fucking whingeing and shut up!' and then run away. He used the shock factor and then he'd wink and smile at you. I said, 'You can't talk to me like that, I'd get booked if I spoke to you that way,' and he'd just say, 'Well, that's what you sound like, you idiot.' And you'd realise how stupid you did sound.

And that's why he was my favourite.

Food for thought: The problem with referees when you're a manager is that you never feel they're going to give you what you want. You don't feel they're impartial and you believe they are biased against you. I couldn't get over that, but I also couldn't see that what I wanted was what I wanted for my own reasons – it was so selfish and so one-way when they are literally trying to be unbiased and impartial.

When I became a player-manager at Bristol Rovers, my record with referees was an absolute disaster.

I was in amongst it as a player and then, as a manager, I was going to board meetings, and I was absorbing all those different kinds of pressures I probably didn't need to. If I was in the board room I'd be hearing, 'If we get knocked out of the FA Cup this weekend, we'll be skint for the rest of the season' – I shouldn't have taken those concerns onto the pitch, but I did. In my first season as Rovers player-manager, I got booked seventeen times. My previous worst had been five. I had to look at what I was doing, on and off the pitch.

What was that saying about me and the way I was behaving? What example was I setting to my players? I was a disciplined person with how I trained and lived my life, but when it came to player management, I'd inadvertently demonstrated that it was OK for my players to argue with referees and behave like a-holes. As a result, our disciplinary record was off the charts.

We were away to Chesterfield in another game, and we got beaten 5–1 and ended up with eight players on the pitch. I was trying to report the referee while he was reporting me for my behaviour and my team's lack of discipline. In that game, I was actually trying to get sent off because I knew that if I was dismissed, the game would be abandoned because you can't continue if one team only has seven players. The ref came from somewhere near Chesterfield and was too local for my liking, but the real problem was me – I was totally feckin' paranoid. It was ridiculous as my players were shouting and arguing all the time and it was embarrassing because we couldn't get the ball in the time that remained. We had to play 4–2–1! Where's Ted Rogers and Dusty Bin when you need them?

I was in a downward spiral with referees, and it got so bad, that when Rovers played Bournemouth at home, we went down to nine men after having two players sent off – unfairly in my opinion – and I was thinking I needed to do something different because we were 1–0 up. So, I went and played centre-half for the last fifteen minutes and we managed to hang on and win the game with nine men. I should have looked at myself after that game and thought about what had just happened because our poor discipline could have cost us three points. I needed to stop arguing all the time because the refs weren't going to change their decisions – it was about dealing with the decisions they had made and dealing with them in a better way.

I had to look at myself and think, 'What on earth's going on?'

But I went to QPR, and nothing much changed. I was an argumentative, disruptive little fecker – I was a little bit like Neil Warnock at the time and if you had a game where you had him in one dugout and me in the other, it was an absolute nightmare for the fourth official. There was one time we had to be separated with a cattle prod because we were going at it so bad. I just couldn't see myself and felt the whole world was against me. I even came home and had a big argument with Kim about a goal that had been given in a game. I had been in a big melee on the ground in front of our goal and in the scramble, the referee said the ball had crossed the line and awarded a goal.

I knew it hadn't crossed the line and argued that it shouldn't have been given. Kim said it was a goal. I said it wasn't and this went on for a few minutes until Kim said, 'Did the referee give the goddamned goal? What was the score in the game?'

'We lost 4–3 and that was the winning goal.'

'So, it was a goal,' she said. 'Was it or was it not a goal?'

'It was a goal. But it didn't cross the line . . .'

'I don't care,' she said. 'It was a goal that didn't go in, but it still counted. Are you going to accept it? You lost . . . so deal with it.'

I had a big problem with justice and fairness, and it was something that's been with me throughout my life. When I was a kid, I was the youngest and my sister got more pocket money than me and my brother got more pocket money than me and I didn't think it was fair. My dad said it was about responsibility and you're always going to get the least money because you don't take responsibility as you're not the oldest. Plus, I wanted to win all the time and if I didn't, all hell broke loose. If I was playing draughts with my dad and I was getting beaten, I'd throw the board up in the air because of my temperament. I grew up thinking that life wasn't fair, and I took that feeling of injustice into football and took it out on referees who I looked at as people who were trying to stop me winning rather than people who were just doing their job.

And then there is the ridiculous amount of times I have been sent off as a manager, and a lot of the times it was because of my reaction to something that had just happened on the pitch or maybe the situation of the game and how important it was.

My biggest strength, I believe, is my empathy for people and the understanding I have of my players and how I try and get them to let me help them with their problems so they can go out and play with as much freedom as possible. So, if I saw them being given an unfair problem on the pitch, 99 times out of 100 I would react – and more often than not, I'd react badly.

I remember at Blackpool when we were away to Birmingham City – a ground I've always enjoyed going to because my teams usually performed well there, and I enjoy the banter with their fans because they're a bit cutting at times and in your face. You've got to walk past all the home fans from the tunnel in the bottom corner of the ground and they all give you a little bit as you go past – and I used to love that.

Barry Ferguson was my captain at the time, and he was almost as fiery as me. A goal-kick for Birmingham, then managed by Chris Hughton, was taken and as Baz was quite good in the air, he used to stand a bit deeper and, on this occasion, he was on the toes of Nikola Zigic – the six-foot-seven Blues striker. We were in a bit of sticky position at the time, and we needed three points badly, so there was a lot at stake. As the ball came out of the sky, Zigic caught Baz in the face with an elbow, so he gave him one back immediately. I asked the fourth official – who looked like he should have had a nappy on – if he had seen what happened. He nodded at me and there was a bit of a scuffle between Zigic and Baz on the ground and then the referee produced a red card – for Barry Ferguson.

I waited for him to produce a second red, but he didn't even book Zigic, so I said to the fourth official, 'You've got to tell him – you've got your earpiece so tell him!'

'Tell him what?'

'That you saw him elbow my player.'

'I thought you were asking me if I saw your player elbow the Birmingham striker,' he said.

'Why would I do that? He elbowed my player first,' I said.

He shrugged his shoulders. 'Oh no, I didn't see that. I don't know what you're talking about.'

Chris Hughton said, 'Well, I saw it. Barry Ferguson got elbowed. That isn't right.'

As my captain walked towards me for an early bath, I said to the fourth official, 'You've got to tell him!'

'No. I'm not going to,' he said. So, I walked back to the dugout and the only thing I could think of doing was booting the dugout with the bottom of my foot with a Jackie Chan-style move. The fourth official saw it and next thing, the referee comes running over and sends me off and tells me I have to leave the pitch.

I'd lost it by that point, and I said, 'You're having a fucking laugh, you absolute feckin' idiot!' I pointed at the fourth official and told the ref, 'This is fucking bollocks, that kid isn't good enough!'

The next thing I knew, what looked like two nightclub bouncers dressed in black with walkie-talkies – Birmingham's security guards – appeared either side of me and I shall never forget the feeling as I had one arm put in my armpit and another very firmly behind my back at my waist as they lifted me off the ground – my little feet were going ten to the dozen and I was thinking 'What the hell?!' I looked like a baby in a mobile walker that's too big for them and their feet don't touch the ground. I was kicking like mad, and it must have looked hilarious. The Birmingham fans were loving it and cheering and then, finally, I saw the funny side of it as well.

Afterwards, I spoke with our CEO Matt Williams who said, 'What are you doing, you fucking idiot?' I explained what had happened and he said it hadn't looked too bad and that he'd try and get me off this time and we'd claim the fourth official was clearly inexperienced. It turned out it had been his first game as a fourth official and I told the whole story to an FA disciplinary panel and explained Chris Hughton had seen it and said it wasn't fair, and for a high-stakes game like that, they should have had a more experienced guy on the line – and I actually got off with that one.

But that feeling of helplessness when I was picked off the ground stayed with me, and now, when my chihuahua won't stop barking at somebody, I just pick him up and lift him off the ground – and he stops barking straight away! I don't mind showing my passion and commitment and think that's

OK, but it doesn't help when you think everything is against you, does it?

I went back to St Andrew's in the play-offs later that season and saw the two security guys again and we had a proper laugh about it. The Blues fans gave me a load of stick – 'You're gonna get carried out on a stretcher this time, Holloway!' and suchlike – but it was just good banter that I enjoyed.

Kim had warned me my reputation had got to the stage where referees expected a tough time and ninety minutes of arguing and complaining, but I thought they'd think it was just part and parcel of their job – that was until I was Plymouth Argyle manager and I realised how bad it had got.

After we'd drawn 1–1 with Mick McCarthy's Wolves at Home Park, I did my post-match reaction and came back to the dressing room. We had people who cleaned the dressing rooms afterwards and one of them came in after cleaning the ref's room and said, 'Look at this, gaffer.' It was the referee's notes and it made for interesting reading.

On the notepaper he'd left behind, it said, 'Wolves: managed by Mick McCarthy, wonderful fella. Really nice on the line, has manners, not a problem. Team well-disciplined . . .' and carried on in a complimentary way about Mick and his team.

Then there were the notes on Plymouth: 'Managed by Ian Holloway – loud-mouthed, argumentative, team has no discipline. Be aware!'

I was absolutely astounded. So, I got straight onto Paul Durkin, the head of referees at the time, and I said, 'Paul, this is what I've just found,' and explained what the notes said. I added, 'He should be turning up unbiased, mate.'

'Er, that can't have been left by one of my referees,' said Durkin.

I said it had and that it had the ref's name on it, too. He told me he would phone him up and I said he'd better do, because I was going to complain about it. In that game, my players had been booked more than Wolves' players had – and they were doing the same things my lads were getting booked for but getting away with it.

So, was it possible he came to Home Park that day with a preconceived idea about how the game was going to go? Durkin said that was impossible.

'No, I'm sorry,' I said, 'he came here ready to book my players based on my previous reputation – you don't even get that if you go into court these days.'

He rang the ref involved and called me back, apologising and said he'd told him that couldn't happen again but that had been his preparation for the game. How can you prepare for a game that you're supposed to be totally unbiased about with comments like the ones he'd made? What you think about each manager should be completely null and void.

Durkin promised it wouldn't happen again and asked if

I could send him the notes as an example of what not to do ahead of a game.

I told him I might keep them because he might just toss them in the wastebin, but he said I was just being silly. So, I sent them off, but I should have kept a photocopy of them just in case.

I wish that had been an isolated incident, but it wasn't. I was at Blackpool a few years later and Kim was sitting in one of the rooms upstairs at the ground waiting for a coffee when the referees' entourage came in. They went for a coffee as well and were chatting as they waited. The ref in charge of the game was Jon Moss and he said to one of his colleagues, 'You'd better watch that dugout today because Ian Holloway's in there. Have you got your earmuffs on? Your ears will be bleeding by the end of today.'

Kim called me after hearing all that and said, 'Be careful today.'

I asked what she meant, and she said, 'The referees. They're already talking about you.'

So, I stormed up there and when I walked in, they were all like, 'Alright Ian? How are you?'

I said, 'You realise that's my wife there?' You should have seen the shock on their faces. I said, 'So, what you've been saying about me, that's not very impartial, is it? And you know what? I've had this before.'

'Ah, you're being too serious,' said Moss.

'Too serious? I'm going to call the head of referees because I don't want you taking the game, because you're obviously biased against me and we're not gonna play.'

I went down and called my chief executive Matt Williams, and he told me not to be 'fucking stupid'. He went on, 'They won't change the referee now, so go and say sorry and have a laugh about it. Fucking idiot.'

So, I went back upstairs and sort of had to eat humble pie, but I would like to thank Jon Moss because he made me look at myself, too, both on and off the pitch and he actually did me a massive favour. I got that one wrong because I was a hot-headed little fecker who reacted first, thought later.

After mulling over everything in my head for a while, I called up Neil Warnock who I was about to play at the weekend and said, 'You're a trained ref aren't you, Neil?'

'Yes I am, Ollie.'

'You still argue a fair bit, don't you?'

'Yeah,' he replied. 'But I don't get in as much trouble as you, do I?'

I asked him why that was, and he told me he'd learned. When I asked what he meant, he said, 'Ollie, I'll tell you after the game. I'll let you in on one of my secrets.'

We were away that day and the game went OK for me and because we'd spoken beforehand, I didn't get into an argument with him this time, and afterwards, I went to see him. I said, 'OK, what's your secret?'

'Right – you need to hear this. My secret is this: butter them up before the game.'

'You what?'

'Butter them up before the game.'

I told him that I didn't understand what that meant, so he took me to the referee's dressing room and asked me to have a look. In there, there were robes, dressing gowns, slippers for when they got out of the shower plus really great food and wine.

'Normally, they don't take the wine,' he said, 'but they can if they want with our compliments. So, I do all those things behind the scenes, and they know that when they come to my ground, they're treated with total and utter respect before the game and after, and they let me get away with murder because of that, I believe. You've got to get a little bit cleverer, son. And when you've done this as long as I have, imagine how many of them I've upset with my antics on the line and how many times I've been up in front of them all, so I've had to learn the hard way. They're only human beings and the truth is, I know how hard it is to referee, because I've done it and you haven't.'

From that moment on, my disciplinary record got a whole lot better. I should have just had the nous to realise it myself a long time before.

I thought I'd put all that to bed for good after that chat with Neil, but against Roy Keane's Sunderland at Bloomfield Road in the FA Cup, everything blew up again and I pretty much returned to my old self.

We had two players sent off at the same time – Rob Edwards for a mis-timed tackle he was trying to make and Ian Evatt, who was shown a second yellow card in the scuffle that followed. They got a free-kick on the edge of the box as well. I'd lost both my centre-halves in the blink of an eye, and they were both walking off at the same time – you don't see that very often, do you? I was thinking, 'What the hell is going on here?' It was an icy pitch around Christmas time, and I was pissed off because in my head, that bias was happening all over again, and nothing had changed. I shouted to the referee that he wasn't taking into account the conditions and that Edwards had slipped as he went to make the tackle, and then Sunderland go and score from the free-kick, so you can imagine where my head's at. I looked over at Roy Keane and he was just smiling, but he wasn't getting involved and why would he? The ref had just given his team the game on a plate.

Instead of shouting and screaming at the fourth official, I had my scarf, my hat and my gloves and as my two players passed me, I took my hat off, unzipped my jacket and took off my scarf and as their winger was running to celebrate, I placed them all by the side of the pitch and as he got near me

I said, 'Here you go kid, they're for you – put them on and keep warm because we only have nine men and you won't be needed that much.'

So, what does the referee do? He comes over and sends me off as well! I asked him on what grounds was he sending me off and he said, 'You're blatantly showing you didn't agree with my decision.'

'What I did was tell him to put them on to keep warm. They weren't on the pitch, so how is that me disagreeing with your decision? I might have put them back on in a few minutes because I was a bit hot under the collar.'

'Just get off,' he said.

I'd tried to make the best of a bad situation and thought it was funny, but the referee hadn't seen it that way. He didn't think it was funny. Roy Keane thought it had been hilarious, me telling his player to put the hat, scarf, and jacket on, and when the ref sent me off, he said, 'You can't do that. Ollie, pick your coat and hat up. He's alright ref.' But the ref wasn't changing his mind and Roy just shook his head. It's crazy, isn't it? I was trying to use laughter as a stress reliever and without being able to laugh and make a joke, I'm not sure what I might have done throughout my career. I can laugh about it now as well, because I know how mad it all was.

I was also fined £9,000 for what I believed was a throw-away comment in a post-match interview during my one season in the Premier League with Blackpool. I said to the interviewer that if the assistant referee felt a particular decision had been correct, then he should visit Specsavers because they had a 2-for-1 offer on and it might help his vision to enable him to see clearly.

I was hauled in front of the FA and told I was bringing the game into disrepute by saying what I'd said, and they fined me £9,000. I said, 'What? How is that £9,000? You're giving me a Premier League fine and I'm not on Premier League wages. I work for fucking Blackpool for Christ's sake! I'll show you my contract – how can you charge me that amount of money?'

How can that be right that I'm fined the same as someone who is on £5 million a year? It should be based on comparative wages, surely? It was heart-breaking and when I went to see Karl Oyston he said, 'It's your mouth, not mine. They're fining you, not me, I didn't tell you to say that, did I?'

I asked him if he thought it was that bad and he said he thought it was funny. Holy Christ alive. Worse still, Specsavers never got in touch and missed a marketing opportunity – they could have paid my fine for me.

Yet again it had all been about that feeling of injustice and unfairness – that's what gets my goat more than anything else. That said, I did improve after that and I don't think I was ever sent off or fined again, so the penny did drop eventually.

Food for thought: *The moral of this story is that referees are just trying to do their jobs and it's a bloody* *difficult thing to do with VAR and all the scrutiny from TV cameras and pundits. You'll get picked up on seemingly the most innocuous action or word and you'll pay the price. And it is so true that when a referee is having a really good day, you don't even know he's out there, do you?*

I'll round this section off with the flipside of referees, albeit from a bygone era, but a nice story all the same.

When I was a player at Bristol Rovers, Bobby Gould told me just before a game that I was going to be captain for the day. I was twenty-one and he told me he wanted to see how I'd handle it. This was a team with World Cup winner Alan Ball in it, and Bally said, 'Don't worry kid, you'll be fine.'

I led the team out and I have to say that the referee was absolutely unbelievable. He could see I was wet behind the ears, and he said, 'How are you, young man? You're captain today, so I want you to toss the coin, catch it and put it on the back of your hand, alright?'

I did it and won the toss and then went to hand the 50p back to him and he said, 'No, that's for you – keep that.' I said I had no pockets and he said to give it back to him, but make sure I got it after the game because it was 'surely your first time as captain.'

He was quite a portly chap who always had a smile and a wink, and we had him an awful lot. He once said to me,

'I know you got there as quick as you could, son, but you need to get there a bit quicker next time, because that's a foul.' I've never forgotten him, but I think you were allowed to referee in a certain way back then and I think that's what's changed for the worse over the years. What's frustrating is that the FA are trying to stereotype a robot into a referee and it ain't ever going to work, because you have to have a personality to be a good referee. You have to be allowed to express your feelings on a game and when you do, with the right authority, it works. You have to stick to your convictions.

The bottom line is the troubles I had, the disagreements and fines, were all because of me, not them. They were trying to do their job and I was trying to do mine, but I lost the feckin' plot, every single time. It's like your kid wanting sugar puffs and getting porridge instead, even though he originally asked for porridge in the first place, and he's gone bananas – again! In the main, being a parent is all about having a little idiot shouting at you all the time, and for referees, that's what managers must be like towards them. I wish I had a reputation like Mick McCarthy – what a lovely man, his teams are well disciplined and all that – but I can't change who I am, can I? I can only work on it.

I'd just like to say sorry to every referee I ever came across, argued with, and caused problems to for being such an a-hole for so long. I'm sure the a-hole status has been bestowed on me by referees across the land – and deservedly so.

15

Working the Chairman

'Are you sure you want me to go, because I could feckin'
die here?'

When I was at Blackpool, the chairman Karl Oyston had a policy about bringing new players in – which basically was that he'd rather take loan players so we didn't have to pay all their wages because we couldn't afford it. 'A lot of clubs have overpaid their players,' he'd say, 'so we'll borrow them for half the money. See if you can work on that.'

So, Gary Penrice managed to get me Seamus Coleman, Barry Bannan, Jonjo Shelvey, DJ Campbell, Callum Mc-Manaman, Tom Ince, Jason Puncheon, Nathan Delfouneso, John Fleck, and Craig Cathcart under those parameters that Karl had set. That ain't bad, is it?

Being able to get that calibre of player to buy-in to what we were doing at Blackpool actually took years of building reputations – our reputation of how we do things and how we treat people – the style of play we promote and how we're going to look after the client, either through the agent or the club itself.

A lot of time, the agent has a big influence on where the player goes on loan, so all this work goes on behind the scenes and has been crafted over time. Then there is the gamble you're going to take because our policy was to get someone from a youth team, a player from a higher league – who was not being given a fair chance, or deemed not good enough – some from lower leagues and then an older player who we'd bring in on a free transfer, so we'd get a balanced group of people. The skill to all of it in terms of management was being patient, knowing what you want in certain positions and to make sure the ones who go out and watch the games for you are really good people because that helps build your reputation of being nice to deal with. And that really makes a big difference.

But it isn't easy, particularly if you're at clubs that don't want to pay agents any money. The part of management that will define you is that you need to get at least seventy-five per cent of your signings right to keep the faith of your owners. If seventy-five per cent of them are wrong for the club and only twenty-five per cent work, you're gonna be out. The owners also want to see an improvement in all the players they already have, because they were sold these players by previous managers who told them they were great and just what the club needed. So, now it's your job to make them as good as the other bloke said they were – otherwise, they'll blame you for that as well!

The whole basis of surviving as a manager is having the right contacts and continually building on them and then nurturing that reputation of looking after players, making them work hard and improving them.

But in football, it's not always about the ones you do get, but the ones that got away, too. And sometimes they were permanent deals as well. At Blackpool, there were one or two we had lined up that were allowed to slip through the net – and one of the biggest was Medhi Benatia and this example is why the club chairman should trust the manager's judgement and not theirs.

Benatia was a young Moroccan centre-half that Gary Penrice had been alerted to by a French agent named Gregory Ducat. I'd been after a young, fresh, fantastic centre-half for some time – I was after a Clarke Carlisle or a Danny Shittu, a player who I knew I could depend on and who would follow me around and be a leader. Pen told me Gregory had got me one, but said I'd have to move fast because a lot of clubs were interested in signing him. I asked where he was currently playing and he told me he was at Clermont and was out of contract in the next few months, but if I moved quickly, it might be possible to buy him immediately.

Pen asked me how quickly I could get over to France because he had a game coming up where I could watch the player for myself. I called Karl, the chairman, and said, 'Look, we've got a chance on this lad who I haven't seen myself yet.'

'Well, I'm not signing him if you've not seen him,' said Karl.

'Pen has seen him and if it was down to me, I'd take a gamble on him.'

'Ollie, with the greatest respect I want *you* to see him, so get out there and see him for yourself.'

The weather was really bad at the time, I arranged the trip, told Pen – who was delighted – and off I went. I arrived at Heathrow and the snow and ice was horrendous and there was doubt around whether the flight would be cancelled. I called Karl.

'Are you sure you want me to go, because I could feckin' die here?'

'Yeah, if you like, let me know how it goes, but I'm just not doing it without you having watched him.'

So, off I went on what was the worst flight of my life. On landing, we skidded all over the runway and when I came through arrivals, Gregory was waiting for me. I was white as a sheet because I don't like flying at the best of times. The flight had been delayed at my end, so I asked Gregory if we'd still make the game and he said not to worry. It was quite a journey, but he assured me the French trains were fast and reliable – and they were, and I felt that much safer on the ground. It had been like *Planes, Trains & Automobiles* and we arrived in Caen with enough time for a meal.

We then headed to the game, and I asked Gregory where we were up to with the player and he said, 'We're in a bit of trouble because Udinese want to sign him on a free in the summer.'

I said that I thought he said we were in a strong position for him, and he told me not to worry because if I came in for him, he'd told Medhi's family that out of the two clubs, he should definitely sign for Blackpool.

Gregory told me to just watch him play first, at the price we'd be paying he was a bargain and not to worry because he'd talked the player into playing for Blackpool.

We went to the game and despite having about five extra layers on, I was still goddamned freezing. The game kicked off and I was surprised by how poor the standard was, because I'd always associated French football with style and panache, but Medhi shone like a beacon. He was that much better than everyone else and he was exactly what I was look-ing for. I watched everything he did, with and without the ball – his actions, behaviours, what his movement was like – because I wanted to get as much information about him as possible. He couldn't have impressed me any more and I was thinking to myself that this kid was absolutely sensational. That was with ten minutes played. I'd made my mind up.

I called Karl and told him I'd found the player we needed.

'What time is it over there?' he said. 'It can only be ten minutes into the game – are you having a laugh? How can you know he's any good after ten minutes?'

'You know what? I've been watching thousands of players for the last ten years and he's as good as all of them if not better.'

'Ring me at the end of the game,' he replied. 'I'm not happy with that.'

We get to the end of the game, the kid had been superb – and I'd known that within that first ten minutes – but it was Karl's money. I called him back and said, 'Right, I'm gonna put you on to his agent and the truth is, he doesn't even want paying for this one.'

'What?'

'He doesn't even want paying – just do the deal.'

I waited for about thirty minutes while Karl spoke to Gregory who then called me back and said, 'We don't have a deal – your chairman doesn't believe what you told him.'

I asked Gregory what Karl had told him and he said, 'I told him [the chairman] that Udinese have a four-year contract waiting for him [Medhi] in the summer and he [the chairman] said he was not going to do a four-year deal. I said the boy will come to you, and he will come now if you buy him now and give him a four-year deal.'

I called Karl up again and he just said, 'No way.'

'OK, offer him two years with a two-year option,' I said.

'What do you mean – that's not four years?'

'Well, it is,' I said, 'because he's that good you'll want to make it four years as soon as you see him.'

'No,' said Karl, 'I'm not gonna do it.'

Dealing with my chairman was never dull, that's for sure. I went for a meal with Gregory, and I told him to let me work on Karl and he told me he couldn't, really. The next morning, I flew back to London on another dodgy flight and by now I was fuming. I got back to Blackpool and headed straight for Karl's office.

He was sitting there laughing. 'How icy was it?'

I told him not to start and he said, 'How do I know Udinese want him?'

'You don't,' I said, 'but the Pozzo family have spent £2 million on scouts and they want him, believe me. I would sign him now anyway because he's the best centre-half I've seen in a long, long time. He was born in 1987, he's a Moroccan international, he's a leader, he looks fantastic, and he would slot right in.'

'Ollie, I'm not giving him a four-year deal.'

I did get what he was saying, because he would have come straight in as one of our highest-earning players which is the sort of thing that can cause problems in the squad, but I was hoping we'd do well, and he'd get a bonus which would almost double his money – but it was all ifs and buts, and that's just how Karl did business.

In the end, we missed out on Medhi Benatia. That summer, where did he go? Udinese. How long was his contract? Four years. Within eighteen months, who signed him? Roma for 13.5 million euros – and we could have had him for 200,000 euros. After winning two titles in Italy, two years later he goes to Bayern Munich – who beat off Manchester City, Chelsea, Barcelona, and Real Madrid to sign him – for 26 million euros.

I was watching the Champions League semi-final and Benatia scored a header, so I called Karl up laughing and said, 'You remember that Benatia? Look at your telly now.'

'What? What are you saying?'

I told him to put the game on and that Benatia – the kid he wouldn't give a four-year deal to – had just scored in the Champions League semi-final.

'I don't care,' he said. 'He might have been shit for us.'

And that's sometimes what you're up against. I was trying to bring a defender who would go on to be one of the most sought-after players in Europe to my Championship side for peanuts and was up against clubs who could offer a lot more than we could, but because of Pen and the contacts we'd built up and how agents and players bought into what we could do for them, we very nearly pulled it off.

It's like a huge Rubik's Cube and if one little piece turns the wrong way, you miss out. If we had Benatia that season, he'd have been phenomenal and going up to the Premier

League would have been like water off a duck's back to him. He'd have probably been sold within eighteen months for maybe fifty times what we paid.

> ***Ollie's Tip:*** *Missing out on players is part and parcel of management – all you can do is sell the club, your vision and yourselves to them, but ultimately the chairman or owner has the final say. And if the player you miss out on makes it big somewhere else, it's never the chairman's fault!*

As for Gregory Ducat, there was another occasion when he brought me a player – and this time, I managed to get him in front of Karl Oyston, which was an achievement in itself.

I needed Hameur Bouazza, who had played for a number of English clubs, but had gone off to play in Turkey where things hadn't turned out well for him. I spoke with Gregory who represented him and asked if he thought he'd come and play for me at Blackpool. He said he would talk to Hameur but added that he wanted to get paid this time as the Benatia deal had been a waste of time for him. It transpired Hameur was up for it, so it was set up for him to join us on a one-year deal. I told Karl and said we were getting him for half his previous wage, but his agent wanted paying or he'd take him elsewhere.

'OK, you know me,' said Karl. 'Get him here and I'll do what I can.'

I knew exactly what he would do – he'd just tell Gregory he wasn't going to pay him. So I told Gregory prior to the meeting, 'Look, bring your player up, sit down with Karl and just smile when he talks. Don't say a thing. Just sit there because you'll panic him, and he'll end up ringing me. Don't talk about your money, because he knows why you're sitting there. He'll tell you this and tell you that and start insulting you – because that's what he does – but all you have to do is sit there with an ordinary smile.'

Karl asked if he was coming and if I'd warned the agent that he wouldn't be paying him and I said I'd already told him, but that he still wanted paying and that he might have to get his hand in his pocket.

Gregory arrived with Hameur, and Karl asked me to show them both into his office, so I did. Then I left them to it. Half-an-hour later, Karl called me and said, 'Something's wrong here, it's not working. I've told him I won't be paying him and he's just sat there – and he's smiling! And he hasn't said a word. I've insulted him, I've slaughtered his player and done all the things I normally do, and he's still smiling at me! It looks like I might have to pay this one. How badly do you need this player?'

I said I needed him badly and he just sighed and said he'd better pay Gregory then.

I drove to the ground and normally after a meeting with the chairman the agent would have left in a huff and be long gone, but when I went into Karl's office, Gregory was still there and there were sandwiches on the desk, and they were laughing and joking. I asked him what he was doing.

'Oh, I like this one!' said Karl.

'Well,' added Gregory, 'Ollie told me what to do.'

'You crafty bastard,' replied Karl but then added, 'Don't worry. I like this fella.'

It was comical, but that's how it was at Blackpool.

Another player we nearly got at Blackpool was playing about twenty-five miles down the Fylde coast at Fleetwood Town – a young striker you might have heard of once or twice by the name of Jamie Vardy – though this was different because we were in competition with Leicester City.

I was good friends with Fleetwood manager Micky Mellon and the second he signed him, he called me up and said, 'Ollie, this kid's going to play for England. You've got to look at him.'

We had drawn Fleetwood in the FA Cup and we beat them 5–1. Vardy scored their goal – and I thought he was electric. Wow.

We tried to do a deal with Fleetwood owner Andrew Pilley who told us of Leicester's interest, and to be fair we'd have most likely lost that battle had we made an attempt. I might have had half a chance because Mickey wanted him to come up the road and play for us, but Leicester ended up paying £1.5 million for him.

And Pen came up with another name that became a Premier League legend when he told me, 'Ollie, you've got to sign this kid.' His name? Olivier Giroud. Montpellier were looking to loan him out and Pen thought we had half a chance. He was twenty-three or twenty-four at that time, but for some reason or other, it didn't happen and he would eventually go to Arsenal where he did pretty well!

Food for thought: But things are changing, and in my opinion, not for the better, either. Ten years ago, it was all about having a network of contacts, scouts and trusted opinion, but now anyone and everyone can subscribe to Wyscout.com and watch a player's last five games on their laptop.

It saves you travelling and all the time and expense that goes with it, but the only problem with that is you don't know what you're really getting; whereas the groundwork Pen and I put in was all about going to see a player in the flesh, watching what he was all about, from his warm-up to how he was with the fans, to find out what his attitude is like; maybe getting to know those who know him and find out a bit more. You can do thousands and thousands of miles and still end up deciding, 'No, I don't like him.'

But sometimes you need a player and need them straight away. At Blackpool, I lost Neil Eardley to injury with fourteen games to go and I needed a right-back, so I asked Pen and he told me Seamus Coleman was available at Everton – I asked if he was match fit and he said he wasn't and that he'd just come back from injury, but he would get fit quickly and could go straight in because he was good enough. He knew Kenny Moyes, Seamus' agent and so I then called David Moyes and he just said, 'Ah yeah, you can have him.' Happy days! Connections. It's so vital.

At Bristol Rovers, I lost Peter Beadle and needed a big striker straight away. We had four possibles on the list and they were all playing the same night, so we had all four watched by different people. Kim and I travelled up to watch Steven Howard, while Pen, Rovers coach Richard Everson and another one of our backroom staff went to other grounds. We had a phone call and I eventually ended up taking a non-league striker from a club in the Midlands. It was something of a panic buy in many ways, but he did so much to help us stay up. The only problem was, he had a non-league attitude, and we had a few issues with him.

I hardly drank at the time, but I knew this lad liked one too many and because he lived near me, I got a call one time from him saying, 'Gaffer, can you come and pick me up because I've lost my car keys.' I asked him what had happened, and he said he hadn't a clue. Halfway there, he called me to say he'd found them. I asked him who that was shouting in the background, and he said, 'Oh, that's my wife – she nearly electrocuted herself because I'd put them in the toaster after having too many last night.'

He was so pure and honest about what he was doing, but he'd nearly blown his missus up! You just never know what you've got in your cupboard, do you?

He was a loveable rogue with a fantastic sense of humour and worth every penny we paid for him, but there is a world of difference between being with a professional club and coming from non-league – at least back then.

I always kept twenty-five per cent of my budget back in case I lost someone with injury. You can put a young player in, but what if he's not ready? You could ruin him.

The list of players Pen had found for me, and I'd bought, was spread over several clubs and the outlay for them was peanuts but the profits were into the many millions – Nathan Ellington, Jason Roberts, Barry Hayles, and dozens of others. I gave Karl Oyston a list of the names we'd made money on at Blackpool, but his response was, 'Why do I want to worry about that when you've made me £150 million in one hit? If you keep finding me all these wonderful players on loan that I can put on half their wages, why would I want to buy any of our own and sign them up for four years?'

I argued that long term we needed our own players, but he just asked 'Why?'

I told him we might not always get the loan players we wanted, but he just said, 'Yeah, but we're doing alright at the minute, aren't we?'

How can you argue with that? That's how Karl was, and I liked him for it, but putting a team together is like a jigsaw puzzle. You buy some, you loan some, you get some in on a free transfer – you don't go to the same shop all the time. You have to mix it and mingle to get the right blend and character. It's not all about how you play – it's about who you are and how much you care about someone else and that's the hardest bit to get right, because if you sign a wrong 'un and you give him more money than he should be paid, you lose everybody else because they'll look at what he's doing, and then come knocking on your door. If you've got it wrong, you're dead.

Ollie's Tip: I hate the phrase 'losing the dressing room', because I don't really believe it is a genuine thing, but you can do that to yourself by signing the wrong player with the wrong character on the wrong money.

You have to have your best player with the best attitude on the best money and everything else takes care of itself, because nobody can knock on your door then. They might try, but you just say, 'Well, when you're worth as much as he is, come and knock on my door. When you score the goals that he does, come back and see me. When you lead the team like he does, come back and let's talk. Thanks a lot, see you. Until then, fuck off.'

All these components are vital to getting it right, and if you do sign the wrong player, the best managers publicly out them and get them moved on straight away. Brian Clough paid at the time a record fee of £1 million for Justin Fashanu and shortly after said, 'I'm not sure this young man is any good,' and promptly moved him on.

We all know the guy in the workplace who is great when the gaffer is around and is full of beans, but once he goes, he puts his shovel down, doesn't do any work, and starts moaning about everything.

He has to be the right player, with a great attitude who can do the job you want him to do and be the person you want him to be. And then you value the people who have brought you these players and you cherish them and look after them as much as you can to keep them on your side.

So, there we have a few stories of 'coulda', 'woulda' and almost definitely 'shoulda' – but there are many, many more.

16

Anger Management

I was grabbed by the throat and pinned against the wall when I first started playing for Rovers – 'Are you fuckin' gonna track back?'

Here's a question for you: If you can't manage yourself, how can you manage somebody else?

The answer is simple. You can't.

My son's got a weird sense of humour, and he said, 'You should watch *RuPaul's Drag Race*, Dad.' So, I did. And at the end of each episode, RuPaul says something which I've sort of hijacked and use myself with my own version, namely, 'If you can't love yourself, how the feck are you going to love somebody else?' The thing is, most drag queens probably don't love themselves as much as they should. Their natural self and flamboyancy have likely been stifled for years and years and I bet that inside, there is anger and some resentment. It proves that you can learn from everyone and take things from the most unlikely sources.

There's a lot of things I don't love about myself, and my wife Kim gets to see them all.

When I was a kid and I didn't get what I wanted, I would kick up a fuss and end up getting sent to my room by my mum or dad. I'd see my mates playing football on the patch of grass opposite our house and I'd want to be there with them, but I was grounded, and it was my fault. I had a big anger issue that was raging inside me, but being so little, I thought anger was helping me, rather than having determination as my driving force. I felt it was OK to get angry because I felt I needed it sometimes, but that's bullshit. It's never OK to get angry because the people around you are having to live through your behaviour and it's totally unacceptable. I got it totally wrong and for years I was unacceptable in front of the person that I love the most, which is Kim. I still do it now, at times, but I'm trying to learn.

It feels like pain is bubbling inside of me and my eyes are gonna pop out. I can get to a traffic jam and be fuming at the wheel, whereas if I can go miles out of my way to get to the same destination, I'm fine – just so long as I keep moving. If not, I feel like I'm wasting time and I'll be like, 'I'm stuck here. Why?' It's not that I'm so selfish that I want to get to where I want without anybody getting in the way. It's the not knowing that kills me. Then when you discover what the problem was, and it was just somebody at the side of the road with their bonnet up or an accident where people had been rubbernecking, it just does my head in.

So, I had anger issues that I needed to address, and I thought that if I dealt with them, I'd be a better manager. I was invited to take part in a TV programme called *Stress Test*. I can tell you now that if I hadn't done that programme, I think I might have self-imploded with my temper. Before I did it, I believed that I was a person who was kind, considerate, and believed in free speech. The anger management expert showed me I was a jumped-up, obnoxious little git who would not listen at home because of what happened at work. If I had carried on the way I was, I would have destroyed everything I had.

I had specialists measuring my cortisone levels during filming and they made me watch something I really enjoyed and then had me painting, and it made me realise how tense I was inside. I couldn't just paint something on a canvas, because I'd spoil it, and by the end, I was just throwing paint at it, and it felt fantastic because I just let go. I suppose it was a bit like that song that goes, 'I've been to paradise, but I've never been to me.'

I discovered that my biggest strength was my empathy with other people. That's something I got from my mum, because my dad was all 'boys don't cry in our house' and all that shit. Empathy has helped me to help others deal with themselves many, many times, but when I try and coach others how to live their lives, I'm actually also saying 'don't do it like I have'. If I talked to my players the way I talk to my inner self, I wouldn't get anything out of anyone because my own self-management isn't right. It never has been – it's always been twisted because I opt for anger over determination.

I've read a lot of books on anger management, and I found it difficult to cope with in my life. Determination is a great thing to have, and you need it in abundance. To be resilient, you need determination, but you don't need anger. After a period out of management, Kim said to me, 'If you're going to do it again, please don't become the result'. I thought about that, and I took it really personally, because I should never be the result. I should be the one saying what we do, looking at what we did, reviewing it and re-doing it if we didn't win. I shouldn't become that result. Think about it. It's a Saturday night, we've had a defeat and I come home and I'm all over it and I look like I'm beaten to my wife because of my mood. I shouldn't have been like that. But it's very difficult to put that aside when you feel the responsibility for the football club, players and supporters with a personality like I have, and over time, I've had to try and curb that.

So, I've tried all sorts of different things, but when you've been in the game for forty-odd years – twenty as a player and twenty as a manager – doing the same thing, it's very difficult to see yourself in your true light. At Bristol Rovers one year, we dropped out of the top six after we'd been in the top two with only ten games to go. My God, if I'd not done the things I did at that time and taken another path, I might have been able to bring success to Bristol Rovers and their fans. I'd have swapped anything to do that, but I couldn't in the fog of my anger.

You can't ask for help as you'd be considered weak and the one big flaw that still exists in football is they help you get physically fit, but they don't help you get mentally fit. You have to go through hell as an apprentice, from the senior pros and how they treat you, what they do and what they say, and you either sink, because you're not strong enough, or you swim back to the top and you're one of them. I was one of the latter. But I wanted to be different, and I chose to treat my younger people a different way – with encouragement. I'd tell them if they did something wrong, but encouraged them first, because that's what I wanted when I was young instead of people screaming and shouting at me. I didn't want to bully anyone – I wanted to be there for them and let them know I was there.

I was grabbed by the throat and pinned against the wall when I first started playing for Rovers.

'Are you fuckin' gonna track back?

'Er, yeah.'

Football still has a lot to learn and a lot to do so I chose to manage in a way I felt would make a difference, not just continue the cycle. I wanted to change the accepted norms.

We're all born; we don't ask to be here but we are. Your mum and dad give you values – if you're lucky – and I feel privileged because not everyone gets that for one reason or another. When I became a parent, I tweaked some of the things that I'd been taught and how things were done because I thought it was a bit harsh. Imagine turning a screw into a piece of wood – I just turned it back half a turn so it wasn't as tight as it had been. I didn't need to be as harsh. I wanted my boy to choose his own path, rather than me tell him what I wanted him to be. My dad died when he was fifty-nine, so he never saw any of the good stuff in my career. Was he proud of me? I don't know because he never once said he was, but after the funeral, one of his bosses called me to say, 'Do you realise how proud your dad was of you?' I met Nigel Clough recently and told him that his dad would have been so proud of him, what he'd achieved and how he was as a man, but added, 'I bet he didn't tell you that, though.' Nigel said, 'Too right he didn't!'

Ollie's Tip: Being a manager is about reassessing yourself all the time and being comfortable with who you are and how you're doing the job – and that's the toughest thing of all to get right. But managing your anger is essential.

17

Dealing with Supporters.
My Way

'Come round to my house and we'll have a fight on the front lawn because I don't think that's fair.'

When I was QPR boss, we got knocked out of the FA Cup by Vauxhall Motors from the Unibond League. We drew at their place, went 1–0 up at Loftus Road but eventually drew 1–1 and then lost 4–3 on penalties. Not a managerial highpoint, I admit, but we were in administration and dealing with all kinds of nonsense off the pitch.

We weren't in a good place as a club at the time and that FA Cup result just about topped it all off. One fan, a taxi driver – a prominent member of our supporters' clubs – rang me up and was moaning so much that I said, 'Look, why don't you come in and have a coffee?' So, he did.

He sat in my office and started by asking 'Why didn't you do that? Why did he do that? Why didn't you try this?' and each time I explained why the things he was suggesting didn't or couldn't happen – all of which were genuine reasons that he accepted and understood when I'd finished.

Then he started moaning about the team I had picked that night, so I got my magnetic board out and all the players' names and said, 'What team would you have picked, then?'

As he went through the players, I had to stop him several times to say, 'he was injured . . . he was suspended . . . injured . . . injured . . . suspended . . .'

By the end of the hour, the team he'd picked from the players available was exactly the same starting eleven I'd chosen to play Vauxhall Motors!

'Hang on a minute – you've had a go at the team I picked, and you've picked the same side!'

It took a moment for him to absorb that before he said, 'Well . . . I can't believe it.'

'Alright, do me a favour then,' I said. 'You're a big player in one of our biggest supporters' clubs – can you just tell them what I've done with you today and can you stop moaning next time because I can do lots of things and I probably would have done all those things you said, but I couldn't because of all those reasons. And if you can't accept that we're not as big and famous as we used to be at this moment in time, you're not helping, are you? Any of you. We've got some young lads, we've gone through administration and we're still QPR, but we're not the QPR that you're used to. So, I'm trying my best, and the biggest laugh is you'd have picked exactly the same goddamned team as me. So, please share that around.'

In fairness, he went back to his supporters' club forum and told them I'd had him in, said I'd been great, and I'd explained the team selection and that I'd spent time with him rather than shouting and bawling at everyone. Apparently, it went down a treat.

Another time at QPR, we were going through a bad patch, but in one particular game during that run we were drawing 0–0 with Cardiff and just about holding firm with seventy-five minutes gone. We ended up losing 4–0 after collapsing like a pack of cards as Rob Earnshaw scored a hat-trick inside fifteen minutes, and I'm standing there watching all this from my technical area when a woman comes out from the stand and up to me from the side. As she approached, I thought back to a few nights before when I'd spoken with my wife Kim about handling any personal abuse that might come my way from fans, and she'd just said, 'Why don't you just reply to whatever they say with, "Yeah, I'm all of that plus a bag of chips." It'll defuse any situation.' God bless her for that! It made me laugh, so I rehearsed it at home and now this woman is right up to me on my shoulder, and she says, 'You're a fucking wanker, Holloway!' and then throws her season ticket at me. I just looked at her and said, 'I tell you what love, I'm all of that and a bag of chips.' I looked back at my bench who were in stitches, but I was just happy

I had a decent comeback, which I'd suggest each and every potential manager has in times of need.

At Plymouth there was a time we were away to Sunderland, and I was so impressed by the number of fans that had made the journey to come and support us, because it had been hard enough for us to get there. There must have been 200 or more who made the trip – and what a trip that is from one end of England to the other. For them to have driven all the way there and all the way back at their own expense was fantastic, and after the game I thanked each and every one of them in my post-match interview and said I'd like to buy them all a pint the next time I saw them.

Shortly after, I got an invite from a working men's club – they told me where they'd be and when, so I went along with Kim, and I bought about ten of them a pint. I'm just glad all 200 of them didn't turn up that night – that would have been one hell of a round! One of them promised to buy me a pint back and when I left Argyle a few months later, he sent me a fiver with a letter saying, 'Ollie, I owe you a drink – have this one on me.'

There was another time at QPR when Paul Furlong had missed a few good chances and our fans had started chanting that he was a Chelsea reject, so after the game I gave an interview to our club website and said to the fans, 'How are you helping? How dare you do that to my player unfairly? You pay your money, and you make your choice, but I'm trying to do things in very difficult circumstances, so I'm standing up for my player. You're picking on him and making it personal and that is absolutely ridiculous. He's missed a couple of chances and I believe he's going to get goals for us, and whoever he's played for in the past is totally irrelevant now. How dare you? If you don't want to shout encouragement at him, you might as well come and shout at me. I want to stand up for Furs, he can't shout back at you, so I'm shouting at you and if you don't like it, come and have a fight with me. Come round to my house and we'll have a fight on the front lawn because I don't think that's fair.'

I put my address out there on the website for anyone that wanted to take me up on it, but nobody did. Of course, Pen came up a week later, worked with Furs, he started scoring again and got us the goal that took us to the play-off final and he never looked back.

Ollie's Tip: I wouldn't always suggest to an up-and-coming manager to put his address out there in the public domain. There could be some messy front lawns to deal with.

Millwall had a way of dealing with away coaches to make sure they got to the ground safely and keeping the Millwall fans away from the main entrance when the visitors got off, but after my time there ended sourly, they seemed to forget those rules and it was a joke that almost cost me my job at QPR.

I returned to the New Den, and I knew it was going to be lively because I'd said some things about certain elements of the Millwall fans that they didn't like – but I'd felt needed to be said – so there were about 2,000 Millwall diehards waiting to give me stick when our team bus arrived.

I put my hands behind ears and was giving it the 'What? What?' and as a result I nearly got sacked by QPR for bringing the game into disrepute. I was accused of goading their fans and I got told off by my chief executive along with a written warning about my future conduct. How bad was that?

They tried to intimidate me, but I don't think they did – and shouting 'c**t!' at me relentlessly didn't really bother me that much. Of course, when my son put out a Tweet later on explaining the literal meaning for what a 'c**t' actually is, I got into trouble for that as well, because it's a blue tick against my name, so I had to ask him to delete that pretty quickly. My lad had spoken to Kim about it, they both thought it was funny and went with it, but the moment I saw it, it was like, 'Oh my God, you've got to take that down.' It was too late, of course, because it was already out there and that was another sackable offence that ended with me having to explain myself to the FA.

Ollie's Tip: The bottom line is that fans can get away with saying whatever they want, but managers can't – so my advice would be that no matter how much you feel aggrieved or think about reacting to provocation, it's just not worth the hassle or the fallout that comes afterwards.

18

Management Myths: Part 2

Bungs, incentives and backhanders – that's the dirty side of the game, isn't it?

Technical areas – what's the point?

Can somebody explain the point of the manager's technical area? I'd love to know, I really would, because during a game, for every top flight manager, the only place they *don't* go is the technical area. Mikel Arteta, Antonio Conte, Pep, Klopp . . . they're never in their box and I think we should be looking at fences if the idea is that the manager has to stay in that marked area.

But why even have them?

I know Alan Pardew and Arsène Wenger almost had a fight once, but incidents like that are as rare as hen's teeth.

And I'll go one further. What's the point of the fourth official? If he's there, ready to take over from the referee, sit him up in the stands away from the bench. He shouldn't be there, and managers shouldn't be allowed to speak to him – if he can't help you, you shouldn't be allowed to moan to him and ask him 'did you see that?' because it's confusing and just ends up in tears all the time.

I remember one of my last games in management with Grimsby Town against Bolton and we had a really experienced referee as the fourth official; the ref was having a shocker and I told the fourth official as much and he said, 'Yeah, he's having one today, he's usually much better than this. He's having a fucking beast.'

We had a good laugh about it, but he said there wasn't much he could do about it because that's not why they're there. I said it would make much more sense if they weren't, because if they're there, you can't help but ask their opinion on incidents you feel the ref has missed or got wrong.

Being a pundit

During pre-season a few years back, I was asked to predict how the final Championship table would look, including who would win promotion and who would go down. So, I did it, and the second it went out, I had loads of fans hating me from every team I'd put at the bottom. The thing was, one of the teams I predicted would go down got promoted!

As a pundit, try not to make predictions, as invariably you will become the enemy of the fans of the teams you think will struggle.

One Aston Villa fan contacted me and said that his little boy hadn't stopped crying after seeing that I'd predicted Villa would finish sixteenth that season – and they did in the end. At least I got one right, but I'm not Nostradamus.

Bungs – do they happen?

Bungs, incentives and backhanders – that's the dirty side of the game, isn't it?

I think the reason we now have chief executives installed at every club is for the owners to know exactly where every penny is going. But football is a business almost unlike any other and how hard would it be, really, to cover up certain transactions or sweeteners?

Everyone has heard the rumours of how certain chairmen had their own turnstile on matchdays. The turnstile that doesn't get accounted for and goes straight into the chairman's pocket – it might not happen as much nowadays, but I think it was probably rife in years gone by. But how could you prove something like that?

It's not something I've ever been aware of at any of the clubs I've played for or managed, but I think it would be a little naïve to think it hasn't ever happened.

Money laundering is not something difficult when you are dealing with large crowds, because is there a really clean way of counting how many people are in there? Especially when there were standing areas and it was harder to gauge the true size of the crowd. We've probably all seen an attendance published that had us all scratching our heads over the years. Just make sure you don't pick the chairman's turnstile on matchdays!

I'm sure that's all been cleaned up now with tickets bought online and all-seater stadiums, but as I say, unless you do a physical head count of everyone who goes in and everyone who comes out, it's almost impossible to authenticate.

On a personal level, there was only one occasion when an agent asked me how much I wanted as part of a deal that would see a player joining us on a free transfer. When he asked, I said, 'I beg your pardon?'

'How much do you want?' he asked.

'I want the player. Why would I want any of my club's money? I don't know what you're on about.'

So, I told the stand-in chairman at the time. 'I'm not sure we should do this deal because his agent has just offered me some money, so make sure you don't pay him anything.'

We still signed the player because he wanted to join us, but the agent didn't get his fee.

It would be an easy thing to do, I'd imagine, but I'd consider it stealing, personally. The last thing any manager wants to do is something that is against the club's best interests, and I would suggest taking money from an agent in any transfer deal is nothing more than biting the hand that feeds you.

It's very difficult in life to always make the right decisions, but I've never turned a blind eye and never would. I've always said it like it is, and that agent probably went around telling other agents not to bother offering me anything or else they'd end up in trouble.

Does it still go on? I have no idea, but I would suggest it does and I think that certain people have found loopholes to be able to do it.

Matchday programme notes

Managers' notes in the matchday programme: not everyone does them, you might be surprised to know. I know of other managers who get their club journalists to write them and then sign them off, and maybe the higher up the pyramid you go, the busier the manager is – but I always wanted to do my own.

To me, being the father of three deaf daughters, words are really important, and I never wanted somebody else putting words in my mouth.

Generally, I'd have a chat over the phone with somebody at the club and they'd tidy them up and send them back for me to approve. I never let any go out without reading them first, and I actually think it is an important communication portal to have with your fans, because it's somewhere you share your feelings about stuff, and it gives you a chance to get across what it is you're trying to achieve.

Never in my career have I sent a side out to get beat, draw or have the attitude of 'we can try' or 'can we nick a win?' It's always been about how we beat the team in front of us, but when things aren't going well, you need to be open and honest without being too destructive to the players because they're maybe not playing that well.

You'll never be fully supported as a manager, you're fighting fires most of the time, and if you ever get a spell where everyone thinks you're brilliant, enjoy those times because you'll feel those flames under your ass more often than not. You need fireproof wellies so you can stamp out the fires that start all around you and plenty of buckets of water to hand – and I used my programme notes as a bucket of water, calming people down when needed.

At QPR, I'm not sure all the fans wanted me as the man to replace Gerry Francis because I didn't have enough experience and I hadn't taken Rovers to where I wanted, so I probably wasn't looked at in the right way when I first arrived. But I think they appreciated the way I was trying to communicate with them, and I believe it's a huge part of the job – and one where you can come unstuck if you get it wrong.

One occasion I did get it wrong was at Palace, when I wrote that I didn't get the rivalry with Brighton. If I'd done my homework and looked into who were Palace's rivals and why, I'd have known the problems they'd had in the past with Brighton and respected their history, because it was quite a horrible thing that happened between both sets of supporters that brought it all about.

Apparently, a Palace fan had taken a severe beating at the hands of a number of Brighton fans some time ago and it nearly killed him – and that's where the rivalry started. OK, it's not a cross-city thing based on location or whatever, but my goodness, I soon discovered that it's as strong as any you'll find in football, and I should have known and understood the intense feelings they had about that.

So, I should have shut my mouth and researched better, because you need to know as much as possible before you start talking about a club or writing to their supporters. I had slippers on at Palace . . . and you don't put fires out with slippers because they have a habit of igniting!

To summarise, I always paid a lot of attention to my programme notes, because I know the scrutiny they get and how many people read them – plus how lines can be picked out and used out of context against you. Your supporters buy the programme, and they want to read what you've said, so I believe the notes are important and you should take the time to communicate with the fans in an open and clear manner.

Transfer war chests

Are transfer war chests real and if so, what do they look like?

Some clubs might operate in different ways to the ones I managed, but if you have a picture of a chairman going into a manager's office ahead of the transfer window with a big trunk of gold coins, that's not quite how it is in reality.

In fact, there was more than one occasion when I had to fight tooth and nail to get a budget of any kind. Just after I was given the Blackpool job by Karl Oyston, he took me over to Latvia to meet the club's co-owner. I was going to meet Valērijs Belokoņs and flew to Riga for what I thought was going to be a friendly chat about my vision for Blackpool, over dinner.

It turned out very differently. It was obvious that Valērijs didn't think I was up to the job. The rest of the meal didn't go too well because I was fuming.

On the way back, we passed Valērijs' bank, which wasn't too far from the hotel. I made a point of remembering the route because Valērijs said he always got to work early – and the next morning, I was up nice and early and was there to meet him as he arrived.

He got out of the car he'd been driven to the bank in and I said, 'Can I have a word, please?'

He said yes and we went into his office inside the bank and sat down.

'I didn't like yesterday,' I said. 'I don't think you're giving me a fair chance. You don't know anything about me, and you've just looked at it and made an assumption.'

So, I explained how I'd managed at Bristol Rovers, what we did and the way we did it and how we'd made them plenty of money. Then I explained how I'd worked at QPR and the restraints we'd had there and how it had really been at Plymouth. Towards the end, Karl and his father, Owen, arrived and again, Karl was laughing and couldn't believe I'd arrived early to put Valērijs straight on one or two things.

I told them that I didn't want the job if I wasn't going to be supported.

About a week later, Valērijs came to Blackpool, and I'd made a list of players I wanted to bring into the squad. The directors huddled in a meeting but things didn't seem to be going the way I'd hoped.

Five minutes later, there's a knock of my door and it's Valērijs.

He asked if he could come in and I said of course and offered him a seat.

'I don't understand. How can you know these players – you haven't seen the players we already have yet,' he said.

'I watched every single game from your last season, and these are the players I want to add.' I then got out a pad with a long list of players' names on it that Gary Penrice, who was helping me out on a sort of freelance basis, and myself had gone through and didn't want.

Then I showed him the list of players who I thought would really help us – my five targets – and explained why they would benefit the team.

He said, 'Can I have a look?' so I slid the pad over to him which had details of their playing record and how much they might cost.

I said, 'I know why I want those five players, because I don't want all of those,' pointing to the list on the pad.

He just looked at me, stood up and went back upstairs.

I thought, 'Christ. What have I done here?'

Ten minutes later, Karl and Matt came down and Karl said, 'I don't know what you've done, or what you said, but you're having all of them.'

By Wednesday, Valērijs had transferred the money we needed and that was that.

So, sometimes you have to fight hard for what you think is right – that might mean telling the owner straight that they are getting it wrong and rolling the dice on the consequences.

In this instance, I had to fight my corner, dispel one or two inaccuracies that had been formed about me and then set my stall out. Would that approach work every time? Probably not. Every club and every owner are completely different, but unless you stand up for yourself and say something's not right, you'll never be the manager you want to be.

I got the players I wanted and moved on the ones I didn't want – and we took Blackpool to the Premier League.

Do managers get rewarded for failure?

As you've probably gathered by now, I have one or two bug-bears about football management that really grind my gears, and the common assumption that managers are rewarded for failure is somewhere near the top of a long list.

It's true that one or two high-profile managers have walked away with sizeable pay-offs, but that is down to the negotiating skills of their agent when the contracts are first drawn up, not a standard, set in stone agreement that applies to one and all.

If a manager is sacked and he has three years left on his deal, he doesn't automatically get those three years' worth of wages in his final pay packet.

Jose Mourinho had reportedly been given big compensation packages after being sacked at a number of clubs, but that's not his fault – his agent put those conditions in because why wouldn't he? And when he left, he was paid what the club had agreed in the first place – is that his fault? No. Is it the club's fault? Absolutely.

The key is what you can agree at the start and the strength of your negotiating power is dependent on how much they want you in the first place. The more desperate the club is to get you to be their manager, the more wriggle room you will get to ensure that you walk away with the best possible financial package when it all ends in tears, which ninety-nine per cent of the time it does.

The day you get your contract, you get your agent or lawyer to look over it plus the League Managers Association and it's all about your pay-off and what is in place if the worst-case scenario comes to fruition.

It's all about protection.

There are loopholes in life and there are loopholes in football, and bit by bit, they will sort themselves out. But how can it be right that I was once put on gardening leave, another manager took my job, and I still hadn't been sorted out yet? That can't be right, can it?

So, managers getting zillions of pounds when they are sacked is, by and large, a total myth and that is something I know from personal experience.

19

Football in a Pandemic

Fans weren't allowed in because it was unsafe,
but how was it that teams still had to play each other
when you're not even supposed to be within two metres
of each other? None of it felt right.

Imagine going to a club having no pre-season, half a team, no money and being in the middle of a global pandemic. Welcome to Blundell Park, Grimsby.

I arrived in late December 2019 and my first season as manager ended nine games early because the League Two season was curtailed as COVID-19 gripped the nation and the rest of the planet.

Our final position was twenty-five points clear of the bottom two and we were eleven points shy of the play-offs.

The 2020/21 season started, and we didn't know if it would continue, so we couldn't do anything, really – we couldn't go abroad, get together in the same room and I only had about eleven players signed on. I'd lost that number over the summer and rebuilding the squad was horrific because there had been no guarantee we'd even begin the new season.

The only place we could meet was at the training ground and our meeting room was only big enough to get six or seven of the lads in at one time because of social distancing. That meant I had to have the same team meeting three times and as my meetings are quite intense, imagine how exhausting that was and fragmented? I was trying to get the same message across to all of them, but it was nearly impossible.

From the last game we'd played before the season was curtailed – a 2–0 win at Scunthorpe – we lost six of the starting XI and two subs. Both goalscorers went, and we couldn't send scouts anywhere to find new players. Add to that the owner telling me he might have to sell the club because he was paying for everything out of his own pocket and just about everything that could go wrong, did go wrong.

Then we discovered we were going to play behind closed doors, so no revenue was being made and everything about Grimsby was hobbled and cobbled from the start.

I was thinking 'how unsafe is this' as we travelled together on a coach to grounds where we had no clue if they were following the government guidelines to the letter. Fans weren't allowed in because it was unsafe, and how was it that teams still had to play each other when you're not even supposed to be within two metres of each other? None of it felt right.

Kim and I were in a bungalow in Grimsby while my family was on the other side of the country near Bristol. Unlike Dominic Cummings, we couldn't travel to see them, and they couldn't travel to see us. We were totally isolated. So, I was thinking, 'What is the point of any of this?'

There was one occasion when Kim and I were walking through a shopping centre in town, and I saw two kids and one of them was eating a chocolate bar when he threw half of it away over his shoulder and into a shop window.

'Oi! You!' I said. 'Go and pick that up! Would you do that in your nan's house? The bin's over there, so go and pick it up, or I will. It's disgusting. You've no pride in your town.'

'Well, this town's a shit-hole,' the kid said.

'It doesn't matter, you've just made it worse.'

He took it quite well, picked it up and put it in the bin, but word somehow got around that Ian Holloway had told this kid off, and the people of Grimsby loved it because they could see I cared about their town. I didn't want it to get out, but it did. It was all about taking pride in your surroundings and trying to make things better, and that's the message I tried to promote at the football club while I was there.

The people of Grimsby are sensational and were great towards me and I hope they knew how well I wanted to do for them. The new guy at the club wanted me to stay, the fans wanted me to stay and work with the new owner, but I wanted to go, Kim wanted to go, and our mind was made up.

Everything was wrong during my time at Grimsby Town and it was, at the time of writing, my last job in football and not the epitaph I wanted.

Getting triallists right

Cutting your cloth accordingly also means you cut corners, take chances and, occasionally, it all goes horribly wrong.

At Grimsby Town, we brought in five non-League trial-lists who'd scored quite a lot of goals for their various clubs, but what happened was absolutely horrendous – and it was all my fault.

It was during the pandemic, which probably explains a lot. Nothing was normal for anyone, including professional footballers, managers and club chairmen. It was also partly due to where Grimsby is, and how far away the nearest decent football club is. The club had found it difficult to attract players, and to hang on to some that did sign for them, because of the perception that it is a bit 'out on a limb'. For a combination of understandable reasons, the chairman was dealing with the agents of these five lads, but I hadn't seen any of them play, which is as far away as you can get from my player recruitment policy over the years.

The chairman wanted the contracts to be agreed before they had the trial so they'd been promised a contract by my club subject to a good trial – imagine how nervous that would have made them feel?

I ended up with one week to have a look at these five players, but we had no games for them to play in because there was still no football happening, so everything I was judging them on was in training. It was an impossible situation for all of us and I ended up signing all five of them because I thought to myself 'he wasn't too bad at that . . . he was OK at this' – I rolled the dice when I shouldn't have done, but I think it's fair to say we all did things that were a bit out of character during the pandemic.

I still hadn't seen them in a competitive game, and when I did. I realised I'd got it horrendously wrong because they weren't ready to play league football, and I just couldn't get them fit enough quickly enough. At the end of the day, I should never have done it that way and instead I should have stuck to my principles.

Now it wasn't a case of when triallists go wrong because it was nothing to do with those lads, it was just the way we went about it as a club.

I'd worked so hard to get four new lads in when I first arrived, to help the ones who were already there – I knew two of them and I was recommended two more youngsters from Burnley – and they all made a huge impact. But they all went back to their clubs during the time there was no football being played and then I lost some of our better players as well during that time. And when you tried to get players to move to Grimsby and live there, it was almost impossible because of the location of the town.

I needed local people with local knowledge to get people in there. Get an academy in place and start to plan long term and that will be vital in years to come for the club, but COVID ruined so much while I was manager of Grimsby.

Your scouting network protects you from times like that, but I found at Grimsby it didn't cover that level and the recruitment policy we had at a very difficult time amounted to no more than a lucky dip.

But there are better triallist stories. Probably the most famous trial story I was involved with was when a young unknown goalkeeper rocked up at Bristol Rovers. I was a player at the time and this lad turned up with a plastic bag with his boots in. He told us that Vi Harris, our tea lady, had told him to come up for a trial. Apparently, she'd been on holiday in Cornwall and seen him playing for a team called St Blazey and had the wherewithal to invite him for a trial – we didn't do things by the book at Rovers!

Gerry Francis said, 'OK, you're a bit late, but go and get changed and we'll see what you can do.'

He came out about ten minutes later and Gerry asked one of his coaches, Des Bulpin, to go over and take a look at him and get somebody to take shots at him. I'll never forget it, about twenty minutes later, Des sprints over to Gerry and says, 'You've got to take a look at him. He's bloody brilliant!'

Gerry went over, watched for five minutes, and then put him in the training game I was playing in, but we couldn't beat him. Then we had a one-on-one session against him where he was again superb and when we finished, Gerry asked him, 'What's your name again, son?'

'Nigel Martyn,' he said. Gerry signed him immediately. We already had a really good goalie in Tim Carter, but Nigel replaced him almost straight away and it was like, 'Where's this fella come from?' It was quite sensational. Two years later he was sold to Crystal Palace for £1 million. Thanks, Vi!

Another time, former Wolves midfielder Kenny Hibbitt was with us at Rovers, and he told Gerry he'd seen this lad playing while he was walking his dog in the park. 'We're a bit short, aren't we?' he said. 'He's a midfielder, works for Goodyear Tyres and said he could come down if you want him to.'

Gerry said, 'Yeah, ask him in, let's have a look.' He came in, looked a player straight away and was signed on. Andy Reece – what a player he turned out to be! It just shows you, you can never say never and if you're good enough, you can always find a way

How to give a right royal bollocking

Management is about occasionally giving out a bollocking, but it's not as simple as just ranting at someone because you don't like something they did.

It's about why you want to give them a bollocking, who it is you're giving a bollocking to, and how they will take it. Have they stepped over your principles? If they have, they need smashing, and we need to go back over those principles again.

There are different ways of delivering a bollocking, and sometimes that means it's not the hairdryer treatment because that doesn't always work – but by the same token, sometimes the hairdryer treatment is exactly what's needed.

You just have to get a feeling and trust yourself that you won't get it wrong.

I wasn't really one for handing out public bollockings if I could help it. If I really wanted to get to someone, I'd have them alone in my office and if they wanted to tell their friends what I'd said, then they could.

I suppose the biggest one I did hand out was while I was at Bristol Rovers and my top scorer, Jamie Cureton asked if he could go out for his birthday after the game on Saturday. As we had a game on the Tuesday night, I had to say, 'That's seventy-two hours Jay, no, I'm sorry I don't want you to do that. Can't you go out after the game on Tuesday because we won't be playing again till Saturday?'

He accepted it and that was that.

We played the game and on the following Sunday evening, I got a call from my physio Phil Kite.

'I know the landlord from The Folly,' said Phil, 'and those lads you said couldn't go out last night, are fucking out tonight!'

'Who? Cureton?'

'No, but there's two of them in The Folly and they've been playing the machine and being abusive. The landlord wants them out. I think it's Foster and Thompson.'

They were my two best centre-halves, and I was fuming, so I got their addresses off Kitey, jumped in my Jaguar, and drove like a bat out of hell. In the meantime, they'd called my house and spoken with Kim saying, 'What's up with the gaffer? He's not coming out to see us, is he?'

Kim said I'd most likely be arriving any moment. At which point I screeched to a halt on the driveway. It was the home of Steve Foster, who I'd brought in from a non-league club, and I went ballistic as I went into his house.

'Who's with you? Who's the other feckin' one? There's two of you, I know!'

He was trying to protect his mate and said there was nobody else there. I went into the kitchen and in the corner was a fridge freezer, with the top door open and the bottom door closed, so I could see the legs of the other feckin' nugget who was hiding behind it!

'Andy feckin' Thompson?!' I knew it was him because he had massive feet.

'How'd you know it was me?' he slurred.

I could have killed them both, there and then, but I had enough wherewithal to just calm myself down and say, 'See you both tomorrow morning, in my office.' I left quietly and drove home.

I've never been so gutted in my life, and I was thinking to myself all night, 'what the feck do I do now?' I'd caught them, red-handed, and we had a game very soon. They were two of the three centre-halves I had, and I couldn't play without them. But they'd broken every rule I had, so how could I play them? What was I going to do?

Kim told me, 'Just sleep on it. You just risked your life driving over there at a ridiculous speed, for God's sake, think about it tomorrow.'

So, I did. And I woke up exactly the same, wondering what the hell I was going to do.

Then I had a flash of inspiration. When I'd first started out in management, I'd spoken to five or six managers for advice about what I needed to learn, and one of them was Watford boss Graham Taylor, so I called him.

He answered, 'Hello son, how are you?'

I told him I had a massive problem and proceeded to explain what had happened and that I didn't know how to handle it.

'I don't think you've got a massive problem at all,' he said. 'I think you've handled it brilliantly up to this point. You caught them, nowhere to hide, you calmed down and you told them you'd see them in the morning. Imagine the sort of night they've had? Now you've got them in the palm of your hand, so you need to decide what sort of manager do you want to be?'

I told him I didn't follow, so he went on, 'Do you want to be vindictive and leave them out? You've told me you can't leave them out because you might lose. What I find works well is naming and shaming in front of the lads. Is there some kind of forfeit they can do, to make them prove they deserve the chance to play because they broke the rules? So, you have to decide what you're going to do and decide what sort of manager you want to be – you've got to be a clever manager because you want them both to play, so think of a way.'

And it came to me – I knew exactly what I was going to do, thanks to Graham's wise words. I had two runs that I put the players through in training, and I decided I'd make them do both in one day, because they're different types of runs with different effort levels.

One was a long one around the outside of the ground – 1,400 metres that they had to do in a certain time, and I had their best times so I could compare – and the other one was a shuttle run. They'd have to do both, and the lads would be there, watching and encouraging. If they didn't get within five seconds of their best times, they weren't playing.

So, we were all in the dressing room and I laid it on them. 'How dare you, I told you, you couldn't go out so you're gonna do both the runs. Jamie, well done, you didn't go out. You, who do think you are? Still think you can go out and drink like you did when you were an amateur? This is a professional football club. Both of you get out there, you've got to get within five seconds of your best time or you're not playing. But I think you're too plastered from last night to be able do it, anyway.'

Unbeknown to me, their teammates set the long run markers but set them deliberately short because they wanted them both to play. They all stood around helping and cheering them on, helping them through it and they did the long run in good time and then I let them recover before doing the sprints and again, they made it inside the right times, so I told them they were fit to travel.

We played the game, won 3–0 and one of the two got man of the match. Afterwards, in the dressing room I said, 'I just wanted to thank you all for allowing these two Herberts the chance to play so well tonight. My gut instinct was that I wasn't going to play you, but you earned the right to play and thank you for proving a point to everybody else. I know those runs are legendary and that you all keep moaning about them because they make you feel tired, but you've proved that the day before a match, you can do both of those runs, and one of you still ended up being the star man. So, I can give you those runs – and any of you those runs – any time I like without you having an excuse that you're too tired.'

Then I walked out.

So, I'd been in a bit of a mess, it looked like they'd totally ignored everything I'd said about going out, but because I'd bought myself some time, and didn't let my gut instinct take over and instead spoke to another manager about the situation because I'd never dealt with that before, I believe I got the right outcome.

One bugbear I do have and always had during my management career was people being late – I can't stand anyone being late. I once heard a story about Roy Keane when he was manager of Sunderland and took them up to the Premier League in his first season. Two of his players were late for the team coach, so they just drove off and left them behind. Nobody was ever late again.

You can go too early with a bollocking, and then you wish you hadn't said it – and I've done that on a number of occasions. When that happens, I use the old 'do, review and redo' technique and I've often thought, 'I got that wrong and I should have handled myself better'. Those are occasions when I let my angry side overtake my educated judgement side.

Ollie's Tip: It's always best to count to ten before you do anything. I know that sounds easy, but it isn't.

All I'm suggesting is that we've all blurted things out and we've all said things we wish we hadn't sometimes, so you have to count to ten – though as a football manager it's normally 100, because it takes that much longer to think clearly and logically in a heated moment.

Some managers never shout or scream. I remember my great friend Ray Wilkins took over as manager for us at QPR and the worst thing he ever said to us was, 'Well, well, that's not what I want. That's not good,' and I was thinking, 'Goddamn it, Ray, we need a hammering, here – that's not hard enough.' But that's as angry as he got. I spoke to his lovely wife the next time I saw her and asked, 'Is he always like that?' and she said, 'No! He wasn't like that when he got home.'

Your emotion has to come out and it has to come out to the people that matter to you, but then you have to make sure that it's not too much because your biggest strength might be your biggest weakness.

But when it comes to what someone's done wrong, you have to deal with how wrong you think that is. You have to deal with how you think that person is going to be able to do it better in the future – not just dress them down – and then it's down to your relationship with them.

20

The Managerial Merry-Go-Round

I know they hate me for that, but I was angry because
one person on the board was disrupting everything . . .

Applying for a manager's job is not like applying for any other sort of work. You won't find an ad on Indeed or a postcard in the local corner shop saying 'Manager wanted! Good rates paid.' We all see the announcements in the press when the new man is unveiled and the press conference that follows, but what about the unsuccessful applicants? You rarely hear about what happens to the ones who didn't get the job.

And there's no application form to fill in – your CV is what you've done so far and that, of course, is out in the public domain for all to see, both successes and failures.

The process of applying for a manager's position is that you have an agent who calls the club up to put your name forward. If you don't hear back, you don't get any feedback as to why, and if you get an interview and don't get the job, you still don't get any feedback.

I had an interview with David Sheepshanks to become the manager of Ipswich Town, but I didn't hear a thing back afterwards, so – typical me – I rang him and asked him 'why didn't you choose me?' I'd been in, given a presentation and he'd asked me about my last job. I thought I'd done OK, but he gave it to somebody else and I thought it was important to understand why. The feedback he gave was that I was too passionate about Queens Park Rangers where I'd been put on gardening leave six months after getting them promoted.

'There's nothing wrong with you, Ian,' he told me. 'I just would have preferred if you'd have spoken about my club more than you actually did. If you have an interview for another job, make sure you speak about the club you're hoping to manage rather than how you felt about the one you had before.'

'In fairness, David – you did ask me.'

'Yes, but in fairness Ian, you went on about it for too long. I would have rather you had just briefly spoken about QPR because obviously you've got some bad feelings about what happened to you there.'

I explained I'd just been trying to show how much I cared about the club and show the passion I have when I'm manager of a club – even though they'd treated me like something you step in when walking in a farmer's field – but it had backfired on that occasion.

Food for thought: I think it's really difficult even to just get in front of somebody and do a presentation – because that's what you have to do these days. So you present yourself, show what you're going to do, and if you've got an academic background you can do it with a laptop or an iPad – and they love that. But when I was in the thick of management maybe a decade ago, it was all about talking about your vision for the club and convincing them that way.

More recently, when Lincoln City were looking for a new manager, I threw my hat in the ring and they said, 'Oh, we have a system of identifying possible candidates and unfortunately, you're not on the list.' They chose Michael Appleton, and I was wondering how they'd come to that decision because when he took my job at Blackpool, he didn't last very long – eleven games in fact – so I was wondering to myself what Michael had, that I hadn't?

'How successful is your feckin' system then, you cheeky bastards!' I thought.

One job I over-researched was Bristol Rovers – and it nearly bloody killed me, but it did the trick. I had to do a presentation for the board, so I wrote out a list of players they still had, what their strengths were and what I was looking for, plus what I was going to bring, how we were going to play and what our ethos would be with me in charge. I did all that within an eight-page dossier with a scouting network of players I'd look to sign – one of whom was Barry Hayles. I explained how I'd set up the youth team to play the same way and did pretty much everything I could.

I created a folder for each of the directors and chairman and put the Bristol Rovers badge on the front – my sister helped me type it all out – and I think I just blew them away because I got the job on the back of it. But I never did that again. Collating everything had been exhausting, but that attention to detail is what some clubs want, and others maybe not.

Another part of the presentation was about the balance of ages that I look for in a squad. I wanted four player groups of four, eight, eight and four: by which I mean four aged 17 to 20; eight aged 21 to 24; eight aged 25 to 29; and four aged 30-plus.

If you have 4-8-8-4 in those age groups, you have a balanced squad, but when I went to Blackpool, they had just one player in the most valuable column – the 25 to 29 range – so there was a lot of work to do when I first went there.

So, you had four young ones – hopefully, a mix of positions – who were good enough to bring in, plus eight between the age of 21 and 24 who you are hopefully going to work on and eventually move on; the 25 to 29 would be the pros who were the most valuable who were sellable and provide a decent income, while the 30-year-olds would be the experienced heads in the group to help guide the younger ones and set the right examples on and off the pitch. The aim was to bring the younger ones through to the 25 to 29 range, Pen would train them, I'd work with them and make them better and then we'd sell them on for good profits.

That was my blueprint and I kept records of all the players we'd brought in, improved, and then sold on. Players like Danny Shittu at QPR who we brought in for £350,000 and sold on for £1.6 million to Watford. Barry Hayles was another – we got him from Stevenage for peanuts at Bristol Rovers and then sold him for £2 million to Fulham; Nathan Ellington came to Rovers for £150,000 and we sold him to Wigan for £1.2 million; Jason Roberts came in from Hayes for £250,000 and Rovers sold him for £2 million . . . and there's plenty more, but that's how I worked and that's how those around me worked.

A lot of it is down to the chemistry with the people who are interviewing you, plus your knowledge of the club itself. A lot of managers are political and understand what the club is all about before they go in because they've done their due diligence – plus they might have someone on the inside who has told them what to say and how to say it. I've never really done that – it's more off the cuff because that's who I am and my attitude was always that you either like me and what I do, or you don't.

When I was on gardening leave at QPR, Plymouth Argyle invited me to come and discuss their managerial vacancy and I told Kim, 'I'll go and meet this lot, but I'll ask them straight about how it's going to be and what they're looking for.'

I got down there, started talking to them and there were five of them all told – the chairman and four directors – and they apologised that one of them couldn't be there because he was on holiday. They said they'd pass on their thoughts to him after the meeting and, if need be, have him meet me another time.

The more I talked with them, the more I wanted the job. Initially, I'd thought that it was too far away – even from Bristol – but it grew on me rapidly and so towards the end of the chat, I started swearing. I didn't realise I was and it must have been nerves or enthusiasm manifesting itself. I told the chairman that I'd heard he was really tight with money and that the supporters called him Staple Wallet rather than Stapleton, so I'd done a bit of homework and had a bit of fun with them, but in the end, I really wanted the job. I liked the look of the squad: Tony Pulis had kept them up but then gone back to Stoke City, but he'd got rid of a lot of the dead wood.

I got a call later asking if I'd come in for a second interview as I was in the final two, so I said I'd be more than happy to. I didn't know who I was up against and still don't to this day – and didn't want to, if I'm honest. I asked if the director who had been on holiday was back yet, but they said he was still away. So, I went back, shared a few more ideas with them – didn't swear this time – and I spoke about possibly getting a bigger runway at the airport because if I could get people to fly down from London, it would make it a far more attractive proposition rather than all the hours on a train or motorway. They had two French players so I said it would be easier for them to get to us from France or Spain than it was driving down from Newcastle. I was using 'us' for obvious effect.

I told them I'd try and use the contacts I had to try and bring in a few really good loan signings and then headed back to Bristol with my fingers crossed. Later on that day, the chairman called me to say I'd got the job and they wanted me to be the next manager of Plymouth Argyle.

However, had I met the missing board member at the interview stage, I'm not sure I would have taken the job in the first place.

It didn't take me long to figure out I didn't like the missing director at all, because I felt he was too pally with the players. He had barbecues with them, went around to their houses and thought he was somebody important when, in my opinion, he wasn't, and I couldn't find one thing I liked about the man. I'd sat in on board meetings at previous clubs because I liked to be across everything and wanted to be there – that's how Bristol Rovers had brought me up, to listen to the board, but I wasn't impressed by anything I saw the 'missing director' do at any board meeting where I was present, and the bottom line was that I didn't trust him. I told him to his face, too.

Sure enough, as time went on, the relationship between me and him got worse and worse. So much so that when two of the board members – who made an awful lot of sense, most of the time – wanted to give me some money to strengthen the squad, he was against it. I'd told the board not to improve Home Park because if we got promoted, they'd have more than enough money to do whatever they wanted. I said we had to build the team first and that I genuinely believed we could get to the Premier League, so that money would be better spent bringing in more quality to the squad.

There was some resistance because Tony Pulis had only just kept them up and I said, 'Look, we're doing really well. We've brought Sylvain Ebanks-Blake from Man United and Scott Sinclair from Chelsea, so we're building something and it's going really well.'

And then our players started attracting attention because of how well we were playing. I got wind of the fact that Pulis was interested in signing David Norris and shortly after I was called in for an emergency board meeting where they told me Stoke had offered £1.5 million for Norris. I said, 'Hang on, at my interview you said you wanted to get promoted, not sell your best players all the time, because I wouldn't have taken the job otherwise, would I? That isn't what I want. I had that at Rovers, and I was in administration at QPR where I had to rebuild the club. You told me you'd always do the best thing to make the team better. How is selling one of our best players at the minute any good for us? Because £1.5 million ain't gonna do us any good, is it? It looks like you're doing the same again.'

'Well, what are you suggesting, then?' asked the chairman.

'I'm suggesting we say no (looking at the 'missing director'). I'm suggesting we then call David Norris in and offer him a better deal, because we know he's worth more than £1.5 million.'

Everyone in the room could see that made sense and were commenting 'ah yes, I can see that, yeah' and such like. Except one.

'No, no . . . that's wrong,' said the 'missing director'.

'How's that?'

'Well, all the other players will be jealous, I know them; I speak to them,' he said.

'Do me a favour mate; the way I would handle that is to say to the player "I just turned £1.5 million down for David. He's got a rise" – which they'll all be happy with because they think the board are tight anyway – "we're building towards the Championship wage structure and he's the first that's gonna get it." Then say to him, "you're not gonna get the same as David, until I turn down £1.5 million for you, because you're not playing as well as him and he deserves the sort of money we're gonna give him".' I told them what they should do about David's wages to keep David happy but also to have an impact on the other players. 'He'll be totally motivated as a result, the lads will think – "well, hang on, the manager's changing the mindset here and we might get promoted".'

I left with the room almost in total agreement that my suggestion made complete sense and I believed that would be the road we went down. But the next time I spoke to the chairman, I learned that not only had the board not agreed with my suggestions but they'd actually taken soundings from a former manager they were still on good terms with, and had done exactly what he'd told them to do.

'Let me get this right, I said. 'You don't want to up David's wages? You don't want to make the club feel like it's moving forward and have a secure, better team like you told me you do? I would have secured his signature because it will get everyone else buzzing because it'd be like – "hang on, I *can* earn that sort of money at this club, now" – the crowds are getting bigger because of how we're doing, but you're not going to listen to me? What's the point of me being your manager, then? I'm not being funny, but you are not listening to me, like you said you would. You said you were going to do what's right for the players and help the team to grow. So, what am I doing, then? It feels like you're still seeing your old girlfriend and you're asking your old love what you should be doing now – this is a new relationship, and I don't understand. I can't have this after Queens Park Rangers.'

I was beyond frustrated, because the reality of life and what I actually did at QPR was that we got relegated when I first went there, we were leaking money, but I took them straight back up and the first season back in the Champion-ship, we finished one place below Gerry Francis who was at Stoke as first-team coach and we did it on a budget that had been more than halved from £5.6 million to £2.4 million. Now that, to me, is managing.

And I'd done it despite having to take all the stick from fans because they were talking about selling Loftus Road and potentially would be sharing a ground with Wimbledon. We had to sign people who didn't have to travel and were local and in doing so found some wonderful QPR people in Kevin Gallen, Steve Palmer and Marc Bircham who came in and played for me and we all pulled together in the same direction.

But now I've got Plymouth Argyle telling me that they wanted to build a team that could challenge for promotion, but they're not going to reward someone who's just seen his value increase from whatever it was prior to Tony Pulis making an offer to take him to Stoke to help them get back to the Premier League.

I asked how they could turn down £1.5 million and not reward the kid. 'That's not what you said you were going to do,' I added.

So, they didn't sell him, and they didn't give him a new

deal, either. That was the beginning of the end for me at Plymouth Argyle. I know they hate me for that, but I was angry because one person on the board was disrupting everything and – in a long-winded and round-the-houses sort of way – going back to the interview and the topic of this chapter, my point is that if the 'missing director' had been present for my first and second interviews, I don't think I'd have ever gone to Plymouth in the first place.

Ollie's Tip: Everyone has to be on the same page at the club, or else it's a house of cards with a strong draught – which you get a lot of in Plymouth – blowing through it. My advice to anyone with a football club is keep the distance between players and owners substantial because it never works otherwise.

Because of how we'd been going, I'd asked for more money for my backroom staff – Gary Penrice, Des Bulpin and Tim Breacker, who'd all come with me to Plymouth from QPR. I was happy on the terms I'd been given, but I wanted to secure my staff with what I felt they should have got when we first arrived, but the club's answer was that they would give me a new improved deal, but they weren't going to look after my staff. And because of that, I got the raving hump and left when I should have stayed. If I'd managed the board better, I could have maybe got them up and been in a much stronger position, but the fact that I knew I didn't have the board's full support didn't feel right.

Plymouth were fourth in the Championship at the time, and we were going so well, I honestly believe that if the board had backed me on Norris and listened to my reasoning, we'd have had a fantastic chance of going up that year, and that would have been some story, wouldn't it? Instead, they went their way, and I went mine because I was mad at them, and it is one of my biggest regrets in management that things panned out the way they did.

I left Plymouth for Leicester City in 2008, but there was no interview process as such. I wasn't aware Leicester even wanted me as their manager, but about three weeks before I got the job, my Plymouth team had beaten them 3–0 and played them off the park. Their chairman, Milan Mandarić was in our boardroom, and while our directors and officials were celebrating the victory, Milan came up and tapped me on the shoulder. 'Well done, young man,' he said.

I thanked him and though he obviously wasn't happy with the result, he was big enough to come and compliment me on the way my team played. Not long after, my agent Rob Segal called me to say that Milan wanted me as his next manager at Leicester. This came at the time when I'd made it clear that I found it difficult to see a future at Plymouth after the David Norris episode and there were also strong rumours that Norwich City were going to make an approach for me

– but the truth is Norwich were never interested and Glenn Roeder eventually took over from Peter Grant (and caretaker Jim Duffy).

So, for Leicester there was no interview – the best sort of appointment any manager could wish for, when the chairman and board want you to be their manager and are prepared to pay compensation for the privilege. The problem was me. Whereas I'd gone into great detail for interviews at previous clubs and knew the squad, the club, the expectations, and their history, I went to Leicester not having a clue about what I was inheriting. I didn't do any homework – nothing – because I went there thinking I could do anything. I'd had the Plymouth players in the palm of my hand, and I believed I could do the same at Leicester.

But the truth is I should have shut my gob, taken Plymouth up and THEN gone back and said, 'Now can you look after my staff?' – but I didn't because my head wasn't right.

There you go, son – job's a good 'un. But they went their way and, not long after, I went mine.

21

Gardening Leave

'Gardening leave? What the hell is that?'

As a manager, I believe the worst situation you could ever experience is to be placed on gardening leave – being paid to stay at home because the club doesn't want you there for whatever reason. For me, that's the biggest kick in the nuts I've ever had in my life. You feel as though you're emasculated and that you've had your tackle cut off.

It happened to me just the once, during my first spell as QPR manager, but that was one time too many and not something I'd ever want to go through again, because I felt I was still doing a good job and didn't deserve it; the players were still with me and playing for me and I was raging about it. Gardening leave basically means you still get paid by the club, because you remain technically under contract, but only until you get another job.

What should happen is that you get sacked and get paid what you're owed, but the whole point of gardening leave is that the club you're with hopes you find another job, so they don't have to pay you anything other than a small percentage of whatever time you had left on your contract. There was no provision in my contract at QPR for me getting sacked, because I had a one-year extension and still had six months of it left. When they told me what they were going to do, I asked them why didn't they let me just finish the season. But they said they wanted the change right then. They'd been looking for a way to get me out and they'd probably just discovered this was an option.

I'd known it had been coming because I'd been summoned three times and I'd always been on a dodgy wicket since the takeover headed up by Gianni Paladini. The first time I received a veiled threat, I told them to wait and see because we'd started the season without a win in six, but I had some of my best players injured. I told the lads the club wanted to me out and they stuck up for me and we started winning.

Paladini would come down to the dressing room and say, 'Ollie, you're living a charmed life, maybe I should try and sack you every week.'

'No thanks, my players like me and so do the fans, so why don't you just shove it and fuck off?'

Those were the sort of conversations we had.

It all came about because we'd been taken over and out of administration after I'd taken the team up to the

Championship. We'd been doing well on the pitch, so the new owners couldn't find an excuse to sack me and not alienate the players and the supporters. They'd felt forced to give me a one-year extension, but said it was on the same money as the year before and if I wasn't happy, that was the offer on the table, and they said I either wanted the job or I didn't. I knew they wanted their own man in, not me, so they waited until halfway through the season until we'd hit a bit of a dip and decided that was the optimum moment to strike.

In the end, Gianni gave it to me bluntly. 'We're putting you on gardening leave.'

'Gardening leave? What the hell is that?'

'You're being paid to stay at home and don't come in,' he replied. 'Don't worry Ollie, you'll get a job. You're a good manager.'

'Well, if I'm that good, why are you not letting me continue with my team?'

To say I was very angry is something of an understatement, and I let them know exactly how I felt. Anyhow, I'm not very good at gardening: I couldn't tell you the difference between a plant and a weed! To me, gardening leave was insulting, and I complained to the League Managers Association that clubs shouldn't be allowed to do that and if you had an agreement, that agreement needs to be settled up. The option to send you home until someone else comes in for you, and you then have to cut a deal, should not exist. I told them to have a go at the FA and close this loophole once and for all. Would the PFA allow a player to be treated like that? That said, I'm sure there are plenty of supporters who believe certain players should be sent on gardening leave . . .

The bottom line is: a club should pay you what they owe you. That's something football needs to look at and the minute a new manager takes your place, you should be immediately paid the money you are owed – or they settle up before they are allowed to get a new manager. That should be the rule.

> ***Ollie's Tip:*** *Essentially you need your agent to agree a deal right from the beginning when you first sign your contract, because it always ends in tears. Agree your compensation in advance for losing your job during the period of employment, with the caveat that it needs to be settled immediately – that's the only way around gardening leave.*

I don't think I was treated particularly well by QPR, either the first time I was there or the second – when Steve McLaren was given the job behind my back – when overall I'd done a fairly good job. I feel pretty calm about it now, but when you're going through it you are in emotional turmoil. It must be like going through a divorce because somebody cheated on their partner, only I didn't feel I did the cheating

– they cheated on me – TWICE. It leaves a horrible taste in your mouth, and it never really leaves you. It's a bit like that old saying: 'Fool me once, shame on you; fool me twice, shame on me; fool me three times, shame on both of us.'

It was a very strange period and a very angry time for me that lasted about three months and as my wife Kim will confirm, I was absolutely horrible. But in the end, I got an interview at Plymouth Argyle, and I thought 'Wow, that's great!' and I no longer cared about the situation with QPR. Once I was offered the job, I had to get my agent to agree my severance with QPR because I obviously couldn't technically have two jobs at once unless I wanted to break every rule in the book.

Gardening leave . . . don't get me started. It's absolute nonsense.

A manager's life is precarious. Or as I prefer to say – prick-hairy-ass. That just about sums it up.

22

Taking Inspiration From Wherever You Can Find It

I went into a shop where they were selling off loads of these little teddy bears for about 20p . . . I bought 22 of them.

I probably learnt more about being a manager from a head-mistress than I did from any of the managers I played under.

My daughters were born profoundly deaf – all three of them – and we didn't know how we were going to cope with that, but over time, we did, and we had to learn quickly. When it came to secondary school, we went to look at Heathlands School in St Albans to consider whether our girls would do well there.

I met the head teacher who was deaf herself, but she could talk as well as me and she was so inspirational it was a joke. She said to me, 'I know that their brain works and their ears don't, so I will get as much out of them as I possibly can and every one of my teachers will have to learn the right way to teach each one of your daughters, because with deafness, one method doesn't work for all and you have to find the right way. My teachers are ready to help your daughters learn and although they're identical twins, they are very, very different and they are unique and the way they learn is unique so we have to find the way.'

Oh my God! When she said that to me, I looked at my own managing techniques and I thought, 'Wow, there's so much more I have to learn about each individual that I'm trying to coach and teach.' From that moment on, I looked at everything I did as a manager with my team and what we could learn along the way.

That shift of thinking on my part was down to Mabel Davis. Heathlands is a school for the deaf with junior and senior sections which have access to all the curriculum that any other child would have, and they assign support teachers to each child, who go into each classroom to help. And thanks to Mabel, my daughter Harriet got nine GCSEs and three A-levels.

Mabel had a picture of a head on her wall with the brain taken out of it and there was an arrow pointing to the brain saying, 'this works' and one to the ears saying, 'these don't'. It was a huge thing and she said she used to point at the ears in the picture and say to children, 'It doesn't matter about these,' then move to the brain and add, 'That's where we're going. You can achieve.'

That lady made the children believe they could do anything and that in turn made me see that with each one of my players, I had to find a way – and find the way that they learned – because not everybody is the same. That will stay with me forever. Isn't it amazing where you can get your inspiration from?

Food for thought: You can search anywhere for something that you can bring in to help a footballer get better. If you look at what clubs are doing now, you have sports scientists, you've got this specialist, that specialist, there is raising awareness of cognitive skills, and much more. You can even improve your peripheral vision – apparently – so as a footballer it's not just about turning your head, but you can actually improve your awareness of what's going on around you.

Team-talks

If I ever got too serious with my players, they'd know that I didn't have confidence about certain things or situations, so I needed to find ways of mixing things up and making them chuckle because I wanted to prove a point.

At Blackpool, we were having a bit of a dodgy spell where the results weren't quite going the way we wanted them to. It was just after Valentine's Day, and I went into a shop where they were selling off loads of these little teddy bears for about 20p each from their original price of maybe £3 each. They were all different colours and I bought 22 of them.

I decided to discard the magnetic tactics board and use the teddies instead – so I cleared the floor and got all the players around while I arranged the teddies into two different teams. We were playing Derby County next, and they played a really specific way, and I could hear the lads saying, 'What's he doing now?'

I wanted to stop Robbie Savage controlling the midfield for Derby and explained he was very disruptive and good at controlling their tempo, so I said, 'What I want you to do, Vaughny [David Vaughan], is take care of him.'

I walked over to the pitch I'd created and booted the teddy that was supposed to be Robbie Savage almost out of the window. I said, 'If we've got our Terminator, Vaughny, taking care of him, then we can just get on with what we need to do.'

I looked around and there was a bit of laughter, a few sniggers, and a few smiles, but we went out and beat Derby by a couple of goals later that week. Brett Ormerod was unplayable that day and he'd probably laughed the loudest at the team talk. Vaughny kept Savage quiet as well, so sometimes you have to find a way to get through to your players and lighten them up enough to perform.

I can't emphasise enough that if you are tense because you want to win and need to win, you lose energy. You need to be relaxed and you have to find ways of relaxing your players in tense situations and I always found it through laughter. If you can laugh and you can smile, it really does help.

23

Believe It or Not!

'If I don't make it back, can you tell my wife I love her?'

Don't kill your staff . . .

At Bristol Rovers, I was fit as a flea. I was player-manager, so I was always expecting the same fitness levels and effort from my players.

On one pre-season run, one of my lads just stopped shy of asking for me to give him the last rites after I probably pushed him too hard.

We set off and ended up going alongside the railway line which opens up into a lovely cycle track, but I set my team off five minutes before I started the race. I warned them if I caught any of them cheating or taking a shortcut, it would mean extra running for the whole group.

I'd given them all a week's warning that we would be doing the challenge, so it wasn't out of the blue and they'd had time to prepare for what was coming. I told them, 'At the age of thirty-seven, I shouldn't be able to catch any of you on a five-mile run if I give you a five-minute start.'

I had my staff – and there weren't many of them – dotted out along the course to observe and check they were doing what they were meant to be doing, but I didn't realise the pressure I was putting them all under, and one lad – Frankie Bennett – who was not the best at long distances, was about to have what he believed was a brush with death. Frankie had been doing extra training to try and make sure he wasn't to blame for any extra penalty sessions and had pushed himself to the limit.

The task was simple.

Run two-and-a-half miles out, touch a particular fence that was the halfway mark, and then run back to the start. What I hadn't realised was they could see me pretty much all the way, so when I set off, they could see me getting closer all the time and they started to panic.

It was all about getting fitter for the upcoming season, but I hadn't realised that Frankie had run himself stupid and by the time I caught up to him, he was on the grass hyperventilating. I phoned our physio Phil Kite to come across and help him. I let him know where he was, and he told me to stay with him and that he was on his way. I said, 'I can't – you've got to come quick. His breathing is OK but I need to make sure I keep account of what the others are doing.'

Kitey said, 'OK, tell him I'll be there in forty seconds.'

I said to Frankie that Kitey was on his way, and he grabbed my arm and said, 'If I don't make it back, can you tell my wife I love her?'

It was hilarious, looking back, but the poor kid thought he was dying when in reality he was just exhausted and Kitey soon managed to get him calmer, and he walked back without any medical attention. Thankfully, he didn't go to the light!

I carried on, managed to catch about a third of them, but quickly realised that it wasn't the way to get them fit by terrorising them. It was about improving their fitness, and in truth five-mile runs or cross-country running has nothing to do with football, but you learn as you go along about what works and what doesn't – and trying to kill your players most definitely doesn't!

How to give horses a team talk

I'd done some filming for Paddy Power with Tony Pulis, with Helen Chamberlain doing a 'Gogglebox' on the Grand National. We were on a sofa and Helen asked me and Tony questions while we picked horses and then talked about why Pu's horses kept winning while mine kept losing, and it all went quite well.

Paddy Power then got back in touch and asked whether I'd do another advert for them. They said they wanted me to do a 'Titans team-talk' to a group of horses who had just run a bad race and I had to get them up for running in the Grand National. They said they'd send the script over to me, but as the race was only a few days away, I didn't have that much time to think about it.

When I saw the script I couldn't stop laughing, so I added a few lines of my own that I thought might work well and I agreed to a day's filming. The night before I was due to go, I realised I had a previous engagement in the evening, so I called up Paddy Power and said I was going to have to pull out. I was a non-runner, if you like.

They were like, 'You've got to do this Ollie, we have a producer and production team all set up and ready to go.' They said they would put me up in a hotel nearby, I'd be done by 5 p.m. and my next engagement was about an hour down the road, so I said I'd do it.

I had to try and learn my lines – which isn't easy when you're not used to it – and the next day, I arrived at an equestrian centre to film the ad. They put me in a green tracksuit and there was a wardrobe lady there and everything. They set up a dressing room inside a riding arena, with enough room for the horses to back into and we started filming. I had three coaches with me who each had a couple of lines and then I had to do my team-talk.

The stable hands then brought the horses in, we did some photographs with me and the horses before the stable hands exited stage left and then I had to say my lines again to the horses.

I can't remember the exact words, but it went something like this: 'Oh, minds elsewhere, are they? Thinking about lying by the beach and then flying off to Kentucky? Thinking about having a cocktail in your fucking hoof? All you modern horses are the same. Blame everyone else if you have a bad race . . . "oh, it was the jockey, oh, it was the trainer – he worked me too hard last week" . . . you never take responsibility. My nan could have run better! And she's dead. And she's not a horse! And she's only got two legs and a bunion. And as for you son, what were you doing in that parade ring just now? Trotting round like Lord Horsey Horse? You want to take a look at yourself in the mirror. Why the long faces? Oh, yeah, you're horses. Now, who wants to go out there and run the race of their lives? This is the Grand National! Don't do it for me, do it for the little old ladies who put a pound on you each way – you know how much that is? That's feckin' two quid! Come on, it's the Grand fucking National!'

I then make my exit, stepping over a pile of horseshit asking, 'Who the fuck did that?'

I'm not expecting Tom Cruise to move over anytime soon, but I thoroughly enjoyed it, and if you ever need to give half-a-dozen horses a pep talk, follow the above to the letter.

Travelling dos and don'ts

There was a time at Plymouth Argyle when we had an important away game at Sunderland so I asked the chairman if we could charter a plane to fly there.

There is nothing worse than being sat on a bus for seven or eight hours for an athlete, both mentally and physically.

He said, 'No, we can't afford that.'

'Well, at least look into it, for Christ's sake. We could sell some seats to fans and that might pay for our expenses. If we do this, we'll have a much better chance of winning because what time are we bloody going to leave to go to Sunderland? We could fly up on the morning, save on hotel and coach costs.'

He looked into it, it wasn't as expensive as he'd imagined and so we did it, with about twenty Argyle fans paying for the privilege of flying on the team plane with us. We went ahead with it, got there in a fraction of the time, we won 3–2 and it was a great flight up and an even better one flying back because our fans were in good voice. I let the lads have a couple of beers and the whole trip had been a great success. We were singing and dancing all the way and my point had been well and truly proven. Sometimes, you have to think about doing things differently in order to get a result.

There was one Argyle fan who was scared of flying, however, and when I heard about it I invited him to come and sit next to me on the flight back to Devon. He said, 'I'm terrified of flying, but I couldn't miss this.' I told him he was like Ted Stryker out of the movie *Airplane!*

The truth was, most away days were a slog from Plymouth, but that's just how it was.

Giving your chairman a 'vote of confidence'

When I was at QPR, Gianni Paladini and his consortium took complete control of the club and as always happens at a football club, it wasn't long before the rumours over the incumbent manager's job started to surface. I had a contract, so I wasn't overly concerned, even when I got the dreaded vote of confidence from the new board.

I wasn't having any of that crap, so I turned the tables and when I was asked about it, I said, 'Actually, I'd like to give the board a vote of confidence instead. They're inexperienced, but I'll give them time to get it right.'

I believe I'm still the only manager to have given the board the confidence vote. They weren't too impressed. One thing was for certain – the situation had to come to a conclusion one way or another. Either way, get your jabs in first and if nothing else, you'll feel better about the world.

Working for Gianni was impossible at times, frustrating but never dull. Case in point: the day he ran into my office where Kim was with me shouting, 'Kim! Kim! They're trying to kill me, they're trying to shoot me!'

So, what had happened? It was the day of an early kick-off at Loftus Road and two men had come to meet Gianni to try and get him to sign a resignation letter – but they hadn't realised that because we had a lunchtime kick-off, there were a lot of people already at the ground, including Kim and myself.

They'd gone to Gianni's office and held him at gunpoint to make him sign the club over and he'd managed to push past them and run out and came to my office screaming for his life. The police were called, and a gun was found stashed in the false ceiling of one of our executive boxes. There were arrests, but after a lengthy court case there was no conviction and Gianni stayed in his position for about eight years.

Do your own homework

I was manager of Grimsby Town, and we were playing away to Tranmere Rovers. I asked a member of my backroom staff to analyse how they played rather than do it myself as I normally did. The end result was he told me Tranmere played a totally different way to the way they actually played. So, I prepared my lads to play a certain way instead of checking the video of their last game myself – if I had, I'd have seen they had a diamond and if you play that formation well, they'll outnumber you in the wide areas.

And Tranmere played the diamond so well.

We went out there expecting something completely different, but as soon as the game started, I thought, 'Oh my God – that's a diamond,' and it was obvious we were immediately being overrun because we had three up front which won't work against that formation.

I tried to change it from the touchline, but my lads didn't understand and by thirty-three minutes, we were 4–0 down. We'd had no practice at playing against that system and we were setting traps, but no one was there, and my lads were playing for the way we'd prepared in training. I'd had an awful feeling beforehand as I sat in the empty stands (at COVID's behind closed door peak) at Prenton Park that something just didn't feel right.

Had we prepared differently, would it have been a different outcome? I'm not sure, because they played so well that day, but when your team is not that good, you spend a lot of time trying to stop the other team from playing. I picked the wrong team and had the wrong players in the wrong positions.

Whether I'd been stitched up or not I'll never be able to say with absolute certainty, but I made sure that staff member didn't analyse anything for Grimsby Town after that.

Dealing with seagull shit

This was a weird one. I was manager of Crystal Palace, and we were in the Championship play-off semi-finals against our biggest rivals Brighton & Hove Albion. We played the first leg at Selhurst Park, drew 0–0 and we lost our main man Glenn Murray to injury.

If I'm being brutally honest, I think their manager felt it was as good as over with his post-match comments, saying that he felt they'd been the better team, his side had a great home record and I think he thought they'd done the hard bit. It was Gus Poyet and he ended by looking into the camera and saying, 'See you next Monday!' I asked my lads if they'd heard what he'd said, at our next training session, and they had – and it had got their goat, that's for sure.

We arrived at the Amex, a lovely stadium which you enter by going through a set of double doors, then very quickly you go through another set of double doors. I was first off the coach, and as I went into the changing rooms, I knew something was up straight away because of the smell.

I went to the toilets and in trap one, I could see underneath the door that someone had spread a load of shit on the floor, the walls and the seat, so it was no accident.

I quickly told the lads that there had been a not very good practical joke played in the toilets. It could have been anyone, even a Brighton supporter for all I knew. What it did, was play right into our hands and I invited the Sky cameras to come in and see it – which I didn't want to do – and asked them 'Is this right?' I then saw Brighton's first-team coach, Charlie Oatway, who I knew, and asked if he could fetch the stadium manager.

He came down after about ten minutes and I took him into the toilet area to show what had happened and asked him to get it cleaned up. I then asked to see his chairman. He said, 'No, there's no need for that. I'll get it sorted.' But I wasn't having any of that and insisted on seeing the Brighton chairman immediately. I was shown upstairs, I went to the chairman and said, 'Whatever happens today, I think we're a better club than you are. We wouldn't have done that to try and put you off and I'm sorry, I like you, I like your club, and I like what you're doing, but somebody has let you down today.'

He told me he would find out who it was, and that the matter would be dealt with.

Wilfried Zaha just sat down in the changing rooms because he was upset, and I said he should go out on the pitch and forget about it. I said, 'Wilf, don't get upset about it mate, just concentrate on your game and if we can win, that proves we're better than them.'

He went out that night and scored both our goals in a 2–0 win. I'd hardly needed to do a team-talk because of what had happened and whoever spread the shit on the toilets – and

only they know who they are because we never found out –
they galvanised us in a way that meant we were never going
to lose that game.

I'd like to just say thank you to whoever it was.

How to get Plymouth a friendly against Real Madrid

I've had some bizarre friendly matches in my career as a
player and a manager, but the best of the lot came when I was
manager of Plymouth.

We'd arranged a week in Austria as part of our pre-season
plans and chosen a nice hotel at a cost of about £23,000. The
chairman wasn't happy about that, I'd had an argument with
him and told him I needed to get the lads away to a different
environment where we were all together and they weren't
going home at night to see their wives where they would
forget what we'd said. We could train three times, feed them
right and we'd have a chance of having a good season.

He was still fuming at the cost – and living up to his
nickname of old Staple Wallet – when I got a call from our
chief executive who said, 'Ollie, I've got a bit of a strange one,
here. Would you move down the road to another hotel for
our pre-season tour?'

I told him I didn't understand, and he said, 'Real Madrid
have just called and said they want to book the hotel we
have booked because apparently, it's their lucky hotel. They

want us to move to a hotel down the road and they'll pay for everything. And they've offered us a game during the seven days we're there because we would have helped them out.'

It was a no-brainer. Our media guy came up to my office for a few comments about it when I arrived at Home Park and said, 'How do you feel about the Real Madrid game?', so I fell off my chair and onto the floor. What else could I do? Because my daughters are deaf, I tend to act reactions out sometimes, so to be asked how I felt, my response was saying, 'I'm speechless, giddy and I've fallen off my chair.' I think he got it.

We went, enjoyed the week, and lost 1–0 to Capello's Real Madrid, who had eight of their first-teamers playing and we only conceded a penalty five minutes from time. What a memory.

Managerial fashion stakes

For an age, I couldn't decide what I wanted to be on the touchline – whether I wore the club tracksuit or wore a suit – and at the end of the day, I was very confused, but you have to find what sits with you best and then go with it. I used to see Kevin Keegan in a tracksuit, and I thought 'that's what I'll wear', because if it's good enough for Kev, it's good enough for Ian Holloway.

Then I decided I felt better in a suit. Then I thought it

didn't feel right swearing in a suit. Then you might lose wearing something and blame it on that or you might win a few games and wear the same clobber. In the end I just thought, 'Bollocks, I'll be who I am and do what's best for me.' So, I started wearing a hat because I've got no hair, and now I've swapped my *Peaky Blinders* hat for a pork pie hat because I like them – and if I like them, why wouldn't I wear one?

The world is full of examples of things we think we shouldn't do because we don't look acceptable to others – but you've got to do it anyway! I would not want to be in a different place than I am right now, because I believe I'm so much happier with who I am now, and so much happier than I've ever been.

I felt being smart was how it should feel to be a manager. On training days, I'd wear my tracksuit because I was working on the pitch, so I put my kit on, I put my boots on, because I had to get involved and that felt right to me. But towards the end of my management career, I wanted to feel smart. I wanted to look smart, and I wanted to wear the club colours.

It's not nice wearing a tie all the time, but I wanted the badge, I wanted the blazer and wherever I went, I wanted to represent my club, so for the last few years, whatever I did, I had the badge on. At first, I'd try and go out with my wife without any club colours so to speak, but come on, that was never going to happen for very long because people recognise me. Plus, I thought if people saw me in club threads, it might sell better.

Sometimes I was given all the gear, sometimes I bought it myself, but I wanted to wear that so when fans saw me in club attire, they knew it was because I was proud to represent them. No matter where I went or what I did, I was representing their club – always. Even if I was out on an anniversary with Kim, I'd make sure I stopped and talked to fans when they came up because I believe that's part of the job.

That's me now, but it wasn't always that way. There was a time when my own clobber was so bad, I ended up being saved by Ray Wilkins.

When I was at QPR, I used to do a lot of my shopping in second-hand shops – and I still do now if I find something I like.

The lads at QPR used to call me 'Sketchley' behind my back because I once drove up from Bristol wearing a suit jacket that had a big crease down the back. They had this thing about folding their clothes over and showing the brand tag, but that wasn't me.

So, Ray came up to me and said, 'What size are you, Ollie?'

I told him 32 waist and 32 leg, plus 38 short in the arms. He said that was his size as well, so I asked why he'd wanted to know.

'I'm having a wardrobe change,' he said. 'I've heard you go to charity shops so have a look and if you don't like them, give them to the second-hand shops. I've got them in my boot so give me your car keys and I'll put them in yours.'

I didn't think about it again until I got home and went to my boot which was full of black plastic bags. It took me two trips to carry them into the house – two on each shoulder – and when I emptied them out, he'd given me six suits and fiteen shirts. Each one of them was a top fashion design such as Yves Saint Laurent, Hugo Boss and loads of others and they all fitted me a treat. So, I went from being the worst-dressed bloke, to the best-dressed bloke in one day. Ray wasn't going to tell anyone, so typical me, when one of the lads complimented me on my new look, I said, 'Yeah, Ray gave it me.'

They didn't believe it, but later on Ray came up and said, 'Ollie, what are you doing?'

'Ray, I'm not too proud to take stuff and I'm not too proud to say thank you. They know I've got four kids, so I can't afford to buy suits like this, can I? So, I'm not embarrassing you mate and if I'm embarrassing myself, I've done it all my life. I really appreciate what you've done and now I've gone from worst dressed to the best in one feckin' day.'

There's no shame in wearing somebody else's clothes. My brother was nine years older than me, and I had to wear his hand-me-downs – even his school stuff, and he went to a different school! I had different school trousers than all the other kids, but I got away with it. And you know what? Some of those shirts lasted my whole playing career.

I told Ray a few years later that if he ever had another wardrobe clear-out, to make sure he sent it my way.

Another time at QPR, I needed a suit at short notice as I'd forgotten to bring the one that I wore on matchdays, so I called into Asda and found a black and grey checked George suit for about £40. I wore it to the ground and Clive Wilson said, 'I like your suit, Ollie, where'd you get it?' He folded the jacket lapel, and it had the George label inside. So, I said, 'It's from Asda,' and he just laughed and said, 'Yeah, sure.'

A bit later he came up and said, 'You did get it from Asda!'

'I know, I told you – there was no need for me to lie about it!' He'd thought it was from some top designer called 'George.'

At Blackpool, I found this beautiful overcoat that I loved, and the lads asked, 'Where did you get that from gaffer?' So, I told them – a second-hand shop – but they weren't having it. But I did – it was from a charity shop in Wimbledon, and I'd had it about six years. It became a thing that whenever they liked something I was wearing, it was almost always a second-hand purchase. They couldn't believe a Premier League manager got his clothes from charity shops, but I did, and Kim and I still love to have a good rummage in those shops on a regular basis.

When I see touchline attire, I know exactly where you are as a manager and I know you're in a good place if, like Pep Guardiola, you're wearing ripped jeans and a t-shirt. He can do what he wants, can't he? But he is who he is and some-times he wears that lucky coat (Gerry Francis had one as well that he wore for a year, even in the boiling hot sun just, because he thought it was lucky).

Killing transfer gossip

I'd replaced John Ward as Bristol Rovers manager in 1996, with John moving across to Bristol City.

We'd brought in Barry Hayles in my first season as man-ager, and he'd scored twenty-six goals in his first year with us. John contacted me to see whether £1.6 million would be enough to take him to Ashton Gate. I actually had Barry with me when the offer came in.

'Do you want to leave us now and go to Bristol City for £1.6 million, because that's what they're offering?'

'No, gaffer, never in a million years,' he replied.

So, I called John and said, 'Hello John, I've got Barry Hayles here with me,' and handed the phone to Barry.

'I don't want to sign for you,' Barry told John. 'I've signed for Ian Holloway, Rovers are going well and if I ever did go, I wouldn't want to sign for a club in your division, it'd be somewhere else, so thank you very much.'

That killed the rumours stone dead!

There's an old saying you'll be well familiar with and that is 'there's never any smoke without fire'.

I've had some weird things happen to me over the years and the first one that comes to mind occurred during my second spell at QPR.

Jimmy Floyd Hasselbaink had just been let go as manager and I was tasked with getting the best out of the players he had brought in and getting the wage bill down. There were rumours we might be put under some sort of transfer embargo because we'd overspent, but they also wanted me to get the team out of the mess they were in and keep them up. I moved on Sebastian Polter back to Germany and didn't replace him because he was on a lot of money; Tjaronn Chery went for about £2 million and Sandro left as well, so the wage bill came down a lot and the books looked much healthier than they had been. In turn, we brought in Ilias Chair and promoted Ryan Manning from the youth team, so we were going OK and though we lost six games on the trot early on, we managed to steady the ship and found ourselves close to mid-table.

By mid-March there were rumours doing the rounds that I was going to be replaced at the end of the season, and these bubbled to the surface at a pre-match press conference ahead of our game against Leeds United. A journalist asked me what I thought, and I said, 'Well, I've got a contract for next season, so I think it's absolutely disgusting, and I'll be straight on the phone to the owners after this.'

Believe It or Not!

It turned out to be true. Steve McLaren had been primed to replace me, and the whole situation was horrendous. All the journalists in Leeds knew before I did! The odd thing is, it had been after a 6–1 defeat against Leeds that I'd been put on gardening leave in my first spell at QPR – what are the odds of it happening again against the same team?

On that occasion, I'd not been getting on with Gianni Paladini but before our game at Elland Road, I had the worst case of diarrhoea I'd ever had in my life, which was due to food poisoning. We'd been doing well and were near the top of the table by now, but it wasn't what the new owners wanted – whoever they were because I never met any of them. I picked a totally different team for that game and travelled separately from the lads, and we had to stop at every motorway services along the way because I couldn't keep off the toilet. I was throwing up and crapping through the eye of a needle and just felt like death warmed up. We ended up getting hammered – after going 1–0 up – and I sort of knew that would be the end.

So, there is always speculation and rumour about your job, and you do feel vulnerable, that's just the way football is.

At Palace, I can't say I didn't deserve to be sacked, because we'd been creaking and you could feel a sort of momentum against you, but I think if I'd been given a bit longer, I'd have been able to turn things around.

My advice would be, if you get caught up in speculation about your job, just do everything you can to ignore it, which is easier to do than you think.

On the flipside, I would never speak to another club while they had a manager in place – that's a rule of mine that I wouldn't ever dream of breaking. Even if I was out of work and was invited to discuss a possible job, if they still had a manager, I wouldn't go and meet them. I would tell them, 'If you get rid of your manager and you're looking for a new one, then we'll talk' – it's just my principles, but unfortunately, not everyone else is the same. Don't do to others that which you wouldn't want done to you! Having been a manager as long as I have, I know what a hard job it is, so going behind someone's back is a non-starter, and my advice is don't do it. Ever.

Ian Holloway and the Temple of Doom

As a manager you get asked to do all kinds of weird and wonderful things that come under the umbrella of representing your club. The strangest I experienced was when Kim and I were invited to a meal at the Iranian embassy when I was QPR boss.

We were struggling as a club at the time and the owners we had were trying to sell it, so I was asked to go to the Iranian ambassador's house in London for dinner where one of the other guests in the room would be a potential investor – though I wouldn't be told who.

It was like an Agatha Christie whodunnit. Or maybe an Agatha Christie who-is-it? I was asked to give a good showing of myself and my young lady as representatives of Queens Park Rangers Football Club. Kim was a bit shy at the time and reluctant to go, but I said, 'You've got to do it, love, and you've got to come with me.' And she did.

So, off we went, and I wasn't sure what to wear so I put on my best suit, shirt and tie and Kim wore a lovely dress, so if nothing else, we looked the part. We arrived in a taxi at this gorgeous house, smack in the middle of London, but we'd arrived a bit early – which apparently is quite rude, though I didn't know that at the time.

We were shown to a downstairs room until they were ready. I always arrived early because I don't like getting anywhere late – it's a bugbear of mine – but we had to wait a good half-an-hour before we were invited to join the other guests.

There were about twenty people there, all very polite and well-spoken but I had no idea who the potential investor was, though I was sure it wasn't the ambassador himself. But the weirdest thing we had to endure was the meal which we were told was fifteen courses! I don't know much about Iranian cuisine, but I was about to get a crash course in dishes to swerve.

It was like the dinner scene in *Indiana Jones and the Temple of Doom*, with one dish being a monkey's head with brains inside, soup with eyes bobbing about – and I'm squeamish as hell at the best of times. There were no live snakes, thank Christ, as I've got a phobia about those, but I didn't want to insult our hosts, so I tried a bit of everything and some of it was nice, but most of it was horrendous. I could understand what contestants on *I'm a Celebrity . . . Get Me Out of Here!* would have to go through.

After dinner, we had drinks and they discussed things like what they thought of our Western traditions and it was all quite interesting. Then, all of a sudden, the ambassador's son came in and he had more of an American accent than Tom Hanks, so I just started laughing. I apologised and the ambassador asked what it was that was making me chuckle, so I said, 'I've just been listening to you all say how proud you are of your own country, your ways and how you do things, and yet your son clearly goes to school in America.'

One of the older guys started laughing as well and I apologised again, but the guy who had laughed said, 'No, Ian, I've said this many times that it is hypocritical to send your son to America.'

The ambassador said he wanted his son to have the best education possible, so I said why couldn't he be educated in Iran? He told me I didn't understand what they were up against and so I laughed again, not meaning to insult him or anything – I just found it funny. At the end, all the ladies went off into one room and the gentlemen went into another, where we had a very large cigar and a whisky.

I was hoping I hadn't let QPR down, but a guy who I'd not really spoken to came over and said, 'I'm the person who is looking to invest in your club – and I'd love to invest if you're in charge, because you sold it to me when you mentioned about his son's accent, and I like someone who says what they feel. Especially if you're a manager.'

Ultimately, he did offer the club some money, but for whatever reason, they didn't accept it. But at least we did our part and if I ever meet Harrison Ford at any point, we'll have some common ground for a good chat.

Unusual job offers

If you're offered a job over the phone, check it's genuine before accepting.

I still don't know for sure if a job I was once offered was genuine or not, but I had suspicions that it was my QPR charman at the time, Gianni Paladini, who was setting me up.

I was called by somebody claiming to be the president of the Nigerian FA, asking if I'd be interested in becoming the Nigerian national team's new head coach.

'The president wouldn't just call me up out of the blue – how did you get my number?'

'But wouldn't you be proud to manage Nigeria?' he said.

I said of course I would, but only after a good career in club management and that I wouldn't dare talk to anybody else while I was in employment without the permission of my bosses. I said, 'Thanks for thinking about me, I'm flattered, but the answer is no.'

They called again, but I was convinced Paladini had set it all up so he could pull me up and say I wanted another job, because he was keen to move me on at the time. It could have been genuine, but my gut told me differently.

Whatever you do, don't get paranoid

I once had a player – I won't name him – who kept on making terrible mistakes and costing us games during a really difficult run. It got so bad that I was convinced he was doing it on purpose.

Gianni Paladini had taken over as chairman with six games of the season remaining and we won promotion, but he didn't give me a new contract. We started the new season with Marc Bircham and Danny Shittu injured and we'd drawn four and lost two of our opening games and I knew Paladini's people didn't really want me as his manager, but he'd begrudgingly given me a one-year extension because of the way the fans were with me.

I was at Loftus Road in my office when I got a call to

go down the road to this hotel and when I arrived, Gianni Paladini and some of the investors were there giving it the large one. He said, 'You can't expect to keep your job, Ollie,' and I said, 'What are you talking about? Birch and Danny will be back soon, and I'll have all my lads and we'll start winning games. I got us back up and halved the budget and we're going to be fine – you haven't seen my proper team yet.'

I went back to the ground where the lads were getting ready for training and said to Birch, 'That wanker's trying to sack me.'

The reaction was that every one of the lads was with me and we won our next four games – all by the scoreline of 3–2 and after being behind in each of them – so everything turned around quickly and Gianni started coming in the dressing room after each win and the lads would be saying to him, 'get out you backstabber' and the like. Kevin Gallen would say, 'Oh, here's Zorro with his sword, lads.'

Our form was decent, and we won seven of our next thirteen games, but the player who had kept making mistakes was still a liability, so I started leaving him out. He came into my office during that time and said, 'It's about the contract I've been promised.'

'Look mate,' I said, 'nobody has been promised a contract – we've just come out of administration and have been taken over.'

'No, no, I've been promised a contract.'

I told him I didn't know what he meant, and said he needed to speak to Gianni. Then I saw that look on his face.

'You mean Gianni Paladini's already promised you a contract?'

He started stammering, trying to cover his tracks so I said I was going to see Sheila our secretary. I said, 'Sheila do you know anything about a contract for (name withheld)?'

'That's really weird,' she said, 'because he kept coming in to ask if I'd written his contract up yet.'

'So he's mentioned this contract to you?'

She nodded, so I said, 'Get Gianni on the phone, will you?' He was downstairs at the time, and I asked him to come to my office where I was waiting with the player in question, and he was so awkward when he came in, it was unreal.

'Gianni, you've not offered him a contract, have you?

In his stereotypical Italian accent he said, 'Er, well yeah, I like him, I like him.'

'I'm the one who gives the contracts out, Gianni. Aren't I? I'm the manager, aren't I? And I'm not sure he can step up, so I don't want to give him a contract.'

'Well, I was just saying to him, hey (name), don't worry, don't worry.'

When the lad left the office, I said to Gianni, 'What's going on? You can't promise a kid a contract. He's made so many mistakes in the last few games that it almost seems deliberate. You've not told him to play badly so we'll lose, and I'll be unpopular with the fans, have you?'

'No, no, my friend, no . . .'

'Don't play games with me. If you want me to go, get rid of me now, but whatever you do, don't try and help my team lose.'

At the end of the day, I can't really believe that any chairman would be so desperate to get rid of a manager that they'd try to weaken their team on the pitch, but once the thought entered my head, I couldn't get rid of it.

The lads told me of a rumour that the lad's agent – who had Gianni written all over him – was like the Tom Hanks character in *Terminal*, waiting and waiting and waiting at the airport until I was sacked. The thing was, this player was very good, but he suddenly started making these awful errors which made me suspicious.

Later on that season, I was placed on gardening leave as Gianni finally got his way and as far as I know, the lad got his contract.

Next up, I'd got so involved in believing Neil Warnock was getting into the referee's head on one occasion, that I got sucked in completely. I've grown to like him more and more over the years – I admire him and his longevity and he's one of the game's great managers. But he knows how to wind people up, and this time I was on the end of it.

I was QPR boss at the time and we'd taken four points from our games with Hull and Ipswich, and I'd been enjoying my usual touchline banter with Neil Warnock. But this would be the first time in all the years we'd had matches against each other that I'd let him get to me, because I usually just laughed at whatever he said.

This time, he was going on at me throughout the game, which we ended up winning, and whenever I questioned a decision, he'd shout to the referee, 'Don't let Ian Holloway run the game!' I laughed it off, but later on he did it again after I said something to a linesman, shouting, 'Don't let him run the game!'

By that point, he'd managed to get my back up.

'Do me a favour, Neil. What the fuck are you on about? The ref's running the game for you – he's made two bad decisions in your favour.'

'Fuck off!' he said.

'What?' I asked. Then I let rip. 'Everyone else in the game is right, you know. You really are a wanker!'

'You what?' he said.

'For years I've stood up for you because everyone reckons that you're a feckin' wanker and I totally agree with them now. You feckin' idiot!'

Just for the record, Neil's name, famously, is an anagram of Colin Wanker, but I shouldn't have let him get to me. I've no beef with Neil whatsoever, never have, never will. He just knows how to wind people up, and the bugger had finally managed to press my buttons that day.

So, was I paranoid? Did I have a case with the chairman's player or with Warnock's mind games? Looking back, I'm not sure I got it right on either occasion.

Effort versus skill – there's only one winner

The whole point about football is that if you're good at it, you've got to commit to it. It's not what you're given at the start, it's what you make out of the skills that you're given and if you don't practise, you're never going to be as good as the skills you've been given.

I think the game is about teaching you what life is all about, which is, you have to put a shift in – and you might do the best shift you've ever done, and it still might not win your side the game because the other team are better than you and you have to work out how you can get better than them next time you play them – and that's the challenge.

And it's not about where you are from or what your culture is, it's about how much you want it and how much you are willing to commit to it. If you keep going, working as hard as you can and practise, practise, practise, there's no limit to how good you can be.

I would welcome anyone into my team provided they wanted to work hard and wanted to win, and I've had arguments with some truly gifted players because I didn't feel they were committing to football enough.

At QPR, Roy Wegerle was one of the most talented footballers I ever played with in my life, but I had a go at him because I didn't believe he was trying hard enough. We'd been 2–0 down to Man City at half-time and after the break, he scored one of the best goals I ever saw as we came back to draw 2–2 – but in that first forty-five, he'd barely broken a sweat and I said as much.

Roy said, 'Oh, the tactics weren't right.'

So, I said, 'Who are you to moan about the tactics? Just go out there and run as hard as you can. Do what Gerry Francis tells you and then add your skill to it.

'The difference is, Roy, you worked your ass off in the second half and ran, chased, and put your foot in. In the first half you didn't try a fucking ounce because you didn't agree with the tactics.'

Our centre-half Alan McDonald stood up and said, 'How dare you say that to Roy Wegerle.'

'Fuck off!' I said. 'You're the captain so you should have been saying that to him instead of me because he hasn't worked as hard as you did in the first half, but you've got a problem because you are letting him get away with it.'

Roy said, 'Sometimes it's just meant to be, Ollie.'

I said, 'Yeah, but isn't it meant to be that you run back and put a foot in as hard as everybody else? I'd rather go back to Bristol because we didn't like losing there, we worked our asses off, there wasn't anyone who was better than *anyone* else and I miss those lads. If this is what playing at the highest level is all about, I don't want it. This is bullshit. If you're in the same team as me we go out and try to win every game, not just one week and not the next. You're meant to chase back and put a foot in all the time.'

Nobody else wanted to say that to him, but he needed to hear it. And sometimes you have to be the one to say it. It's not about who you are or where you are from – just what you do, and for me in my management career, it was all about mentality and attitude.

No matter how much you want something, football doesn't give it you for free and just when you think you've got it all, it takes it all away from you – and that's how it is, that's the game and that's what is so wonderful about it.

It teaches you so much about life and I'm so glad I've been able to meet so many different people from so many different backgrounds. It is absolutely incredible, but you have to give it everything and be the best that you can be, and only then will l have you in my team.

24

The Crème de la Crème

'Son, always keep your dignity, because things invariably
go pear-shaped . . .'

Managing in football is a privilege and I admire anyone who
has ever had a go. I've been inspired by so many in my lifetime, it's hard to know where to start, but I'll give it a try.

When I was growing up and was a player, Brian Clough
fascinated me, totally and utterly. Not just for his achieve-
ments, either, but because of how outspoken he was and the
way he did things which was totally unique. I never believed
enough in myself to actually brag about anything I'd done, so,
anybody who made it known that they were good to whoever
would listen, I couldn't get over that.

Cloughie was a real inspiration for me and so was
Muhammad Ali – I've a tattoo of him on my arm – because
part of me wished I was like they were and if I could start
again, knowing what I did and what I managed to do, it
would have been a lot easier, and I'd have had a lot more
belief about myself.

I also feel privileged to have managed in an era when I've seen Sir Alex Ferguson build up a Manchester United side that were trying to emulate Liverpool's past successes – and achieving it.

Also, to have managed during a time when Arsène Wenger arrived and the way his philosophy changed the game over here was an honour. He brought a new mentality and levels of fitness we'd never experienced before and ended a drinking culture that was rife in English football and particularly at Arsenal where players drank too much and still believed they could run it off the next day. He changed all of that and you have to look at Arsène and Sir Alex for being great in their own ways and competing against each other, building teams that won trophy after trophy. Their longevity is something I don't think we'll ever see again.

I only once was on the end of a Sir Alex hairdryer moment, but it sort of ended amicably. I was Blackpool manager at the time, and we'd just played Peterborough who were managed by his son, Darren. Peterborough had just taken on loan a really good United player and I said I thought Darren was a good manager in his own right, but it was very difficult to walk in a great man's shoes. I also said, 'But if my dad was a manager of a club like Manchester United and I could loan a centre-forward like that, it's gonna help, isn't it?'

I'm not sure if it was Darren or Sir Alex who took umbrage at that, but not long after I got a voice message from

Sir Alex. He was raging, shouting and screaming down the phone at me.

I called him back straight away, 'That's not what I said. All I said was Darren's a very good manager and I wish I could have loaned your player because he's great and I wish my dad was as good as you.'

'Oh alright,' he said. 'It's just Darren was a bit upset about it, that's all.'

'OK, I'll have a word with Darren when I see him next.'

You can walk a fine line with other managers sometimes, as I discovered with Neil Warnock and Mick McCarthy in those little misunderstandings you read about earlier in the book.

Kenny Dalglish is an absolute hero of mine and so I cannot fail to mention Sir Kenny. I first met him at a League Managers Association dinner and we'd just been on holiday in Scotland listening to his audio book in the car and it was like he was in the back seat! It was pouring with rain, but it didn't matter because it felt like the sun was shining in the car. He was the best footballer I ever saw and looking at what he did as a player-manager at Liverpool and then going to Blackburn and winning the Premier League title was incredible.

I saw him across the room, and I said to Kim, 'Should I go across and speak to him or not?' She told me to go over, and I did. I said, 'Hello Ken,' and he went, 'Hello, son! How are you?'

'Great Ken, thanks. Can I have your autograph?'

'You're having a laugh, aren't you?' He thought I was talking the piss.

'No, it's just I'm a huge fan of yours.'

He still thought I was joking, but eventually he realised I meant it and did it for me. I asked him how he combined being a player and a manager at Liverpool to such a high standard, winning all the trophies he did, because I'd found it difficult to do that at Bristol Rovers, and he just smiled.

'With the staff I had at Liverpool, it was easy. They'd just tell me to train, and they'd sort everything else out.' He had Ronnie Moran and Roy Evans there, he said it was thanks to them and not him.

I said he didn't have them at Blackburn Rovers, but he said he just had a wonderful owner there. That was Kenny – he never took credit for any of it, which is a measure of the man and why I hold him in such high regard.

I must have been having a bit of a moan up because I think I was on gardening leave at QPR at the time and he said, 'Son, always keep your dignity, because things always go pear-shaped. You've always done that, so make sure you keep your dignity and keep doing it.'

Sometimes you meet your heroes, and they don't live up to your expectations, but with Kenny Dalglish, it was the opposite. An absolutely fantastic fella.

I'd have to say Kevin Keegan, in his own way, was another

total inspiration, managing his teams to play in such an attacking, entertaining style – plus for that wonderful rant at Sir Alex when he said, 'I'd luv it, luv it!' King Kev wore his heart on his sleeve, ran on pure adrenaline and emotion and I took a lot from the fact he'd started at a lower league club in Scunthorpe United, but went on to achieve everything he did and be so sensational for Liverpool – and then go and do it again in Germany with Hamburg. Absolutely outstanding, wasn't it?

Then there's Jose Mourinho and what he did with Porto before coming over here with Chelsea and claiming to be the 'Special One'- I was like, wow! And part of me wanted him to fall flat on his face for saying that, but he didn't, and he looked almost invincible for a time, but football started changing and who'd have thought he would go quite a while without winning anything or go off the boil and not be as coveted as he once was? It's quite incredible how things can change so quickly in management. I've learned so much from him about the game – he was a real student of coaching, taking almost every badge you can do throughout the conti-nent. He's a pure lover of football and he has inspired me on many different levels throughout his career.

Gerry Francis was one of my first inspirations because he taught me how to get better and he showed me, in front of my own eyes, how good you can be. Gerry and Kenny Hibbitt on our training ground playing against us was like 'Oh my

God – look how good they are, look at their touch, look at their vision' – and they were thirty-six at the time. Gerry and Ken would say, 'you can do this' and I'll be forever thankful for them coming into my life and for taking me back to Bristol Rovers at that time. To have those two around me every day was something else, it really was.

It was Gerry who took me up to the top flight with QPR as well, because at twenty-nine I didn't think I was ever going to get there. He took me from Bristol Rovers, and I'd been playing for eleven years at senior level by that time and had five great years with the Rs thanks to his belief in me and for helping me believe I was good enough to play at that standard.

Ray Wilkins – what a player and what a fantastic man he was. He was a teammate first and also my manager for a short while and he doubled my money at QPR because he valued me so highly, and I don't think I need to spell out what that did for my confidence. So, I shall be forever thankful to Razor, who is sadly missed in football.

My message to people from all my years as a manager? I'd highly recommend it and if you ever get the chance to manage a football club, take it because it helps you immensely in your life. It helps you look at yourself; you can't be a manager and look after someone else if you can't look after yourself first. Management, I believe, makes you a better person. Chances to be a manager are few and far between and it's getting harder and harder, and you're not given as long as you should be given, but if the opportunity arises, go for it, because it's a fantastic challenge.

Once you've been a manager, you're never really finished, and you always leave the door open because you miss it when you're not doing it. You get so much out of it, so you would always consider doing it again. For instance, how many times has Neil Warnock retired? He probably still wants to manage now as I write this (July 2022)! Roy Hodgson is another example, and their longevity is quite incredible. But I get it. I know why they do what they do.

Part of me always thought Sir Alex would return at Man United – and maybe he should. Christ knows, if they keep going the way they have been, he might well have to.

Putting what management is into words is almost impossible. The pain, the joy, the frustration, the elation, the satisfaction, the disappointment . . . it's all wrapped up in one experience and it really comes down to three words – winning, drawing, losing – that's what it's all about and you have to learn to deal with those three outcomes. At the end of the day, you'll never crack football – it will turn around and bite you on the backside. It always does.

Football is an acceleration of life. By that I mean it gives you all the emotions that life does, but it can do it in just one week. What else even comes close? That Aguero moment for Man City in 2012 – what else in life could create that kind of unbridled joy and emotion?

The Crème de la Crème

There have been some wonderful writers and brilliant filmmakers over the years, but none of them come close to the drama that football can give you and it happens on a regular basis.

It's like a drug and when you've done it once, you're addicted for life.

Acknowledgements

The problem with acknowledgments pages is there is always the chance you will unintentionally miss somebody – or some people – out. But I would like to thank Headline for publishing this book and giving me this unique opportunity. I know there are a lot of people involved in the publishing process, but a big thanks to my editor Jonathan Taylor for his patience, guidance and expertise and, of course, to my ghostwriter David Clayton who always manages to capture my voice on the written page.

If I listed each and every person who I've taken something from, learned off or who has influenced me in one way or another, we'd be here all night, Besides, it's not just people in football that have inspired me along the way. There's just too many.

With that in mind, I'm going to keep this fairly simple.

My wife Kim embodies everything that our life together has been all about – and I'm talking about her fight and determination every step of the way to get over cancer.

We got married and wanted kids, but when she was diagnosed, the doctors told us she might not be able to have any children, yet we went on to have three daughters and a son and today we have seven grandchildren, and I believe it's all down to her wonderful way of coping with things.

She dealt with all of that, and I just followed.

Of course, I've had many marvellous people in my life, it's just that there's one that stands out over everyone else, and that's the woman I want to share the rest of my life with.

I suppose my life has been a journey involving many different people – and it was about trying to understand them, trying to live with them, work with them and understand where they are and learn where I fit in, plus how I can help them and what they can do to help me.

In life, you have to adapt, evolve and overcome adversity, and the one person I've seen do that with my own eyes – and do it in such a beautiful, wonderful way that's totally inspired me – is Kim.

What I've learned is that life is all about getting up when you've been knocked down, dusting yourself down, and going again.

I was always able to get back up again, and the only reason I could was because a wonderful woman taught me how.

In life, you should never give in.

I've had people influence me that don't even know it. I watch them in adversity, maybe coping with some natural disaster or whatever and I'm thinking, 'My God, how are you coping with that?'

The pandemic has changed the way a lot of people think, and I'm one of them. When you're in the game, whether that's as a manager or as a player, you think you are so important – but you're not. You're just the entertainment. It's not needed and it's not essential; not like somebody delivering food to a vulnerable person during lockdown to help them survive.

If you don't eat, you won't be here whereas if you don't watch a game, you'll get by just fine.

Football is a choice and I hope it's around for as long as people keep enjoying it, but for me, life is about understanding and growing through the game I love the most.

This is a book about football management and it's about helping those who might want to give it a go, and I hope it gives an insight into a crazy, chaotic and wonderful job.

So, thanks to everyone who inspired me along the way. You know who you are – even if some of you don't.

Index

academy 20
Adam, Charlie 84, 123, 131–7
Adams, Mickey 43
advice 91–2
AFC Wimbledon 91, 147–8
agents 69, 72, 145, 170, 172–3, 174,
    201, 208, 213, 241
    contract negotiations 126–30,
        133–4, 135
    managerial appointments 224
    and player acquisitions 52–4
Ainsworth, Gareth 35–6, 41
Allardyce, Sam 21, 116
anger management 185–90
Appleton, Michael 226
Arsenal 52, 84, 117–18, 180, 281
Arteta, Mikel 198
Aston Villa 83–5, 200
attitude 95, 278
Austria 259–60
authenticity 105, 141
awareness 245

Ba, Demba 11
Ball, Alan 167
ballet training 59
Barcelona 99
Barker, Simon 77
Barrow 90
Barton, Joey, drops shorts 141–2
Bassett, Dave (Harry) xii, 30, 45, 80

Bayern Munich 176
Beadle, Peter 181–2
Belokoņs, Valērijs 205–7
Benatia, Medhi 171–7
Bendtner, Nicklas 52–3
Bennett, Frankie, death scare 249–50
Bircham, Marc 35–7, 38, 41, 234, 272,
    273
Bird, Graham 14
Blackpool 16–17, 18, 21, 45, 100, 113,
    140–1, 161–6, 227, 264, 281–2
    Adam contract negotiations
        131–7
    Bouazza signing 177–9
    coaching staff 18–19
    food for thought 17
    golf day 59
    loan players 169–70, 182–3
    miss Benatia 171–7, 172–3
    missed players 181
    promotion to the Premier League
        82–6, 117–20, 133
    relegation 119, 137
    room service incident 25–8
    team-talks 245–7
    top of the Premier League 117
    training 59
    training ground 24–5
    transfer war chests 205–8
    Vardy signing 179–80
    vs Aston Villa 83–5

Index

vs Birmingham City 156–9
vs Manchester United 122–3
vs Tottenham 83, 85–6
blame 8
blunt talk 53–4
board members
    relationship with 228–36
    vote of confidence 254–5
body language 2
Bolasie, Yannick 144
bollockings 217–23
Bolton Wanderers 21, 116, 199
bookings 152
Bouazza, Hameur 177–9
boundaries 4
Bournemouth 153–4
Bowen, Graham 128–9
Boxing Day 73–4, 74
Breacker, Tim 18, 235
Brentford 30
Brighton & Hove Albion 204, 257–9
Bristol City 104, 265
Bristol Rovers xi–xiv, 206
    bollockings 217–22
    Christmas Day 74
    Ellington signing 70–2
    Harris signing 215–16
    IH as captain 167–8
    IH's appointment 226–8
    press conferences 139–40, 140,
        146–7
    and referees 152–4
    Stewart contract negotiations
        126–31
    training 106–7, 111–12, 248–50
    transfer gossip 265
    vs Notts County 116
    young players 189–90
Brown, Phil 90, 102, 105
Bullard, Jimmy 102
Bulpin, Des 18, 216, 235
bungs 200–2
Burnley 89, 215

camaraderie 31, 40, 59
Campbell, DJ 134

Canfield, Jack 6–9
Carabao Cup 85–6
Cardiff 193–4
care 72, 150
caretaker managers 89–91
Carlisle, Clarke 147, 148–50, 171
Carter, Tim 215–16
Cascades 44
centre-forwards 106–14
    confidence 107
    fitness 110
    mindset 109, 111–12
    Ollie's Tip 110
    position-specific training 106–13
Chair, Ilias 266
chairman's players 272–5
chairmen 52–7, 64, 66, 69–70, 85,
        95–6, 126, 145, 213–14
    dealing with 175
    faith in manager 170
    food for thought 180
    never their fault 177
    Ollie's Tips 177, 183
    players 272–5
    supporting 254–5
    turnstile 200
    working with 169–84
Chamberlain, Helen 250
Champions League 21, 44, 99, 176
character, testing 31–2
Charlton, Bobby 146
Charlton Athletic 90–1
Chelsea 11, 18, 99, 284
Chery, Tjaronn 266
Chesterfield 153
chief executives 51, 126
chief scout 14
Christmas 72–5
Christmas fixtures 72–4
circuit-breakers 58–9
Claremont 171–6
clothes 260–5
Clough, Brian 63, 117, 184, 190, 280
Clough, Nigel 190
club attire 261–2
club colours, wearing 261–2

Index

club philosophy 91
coaching 47–62
  defence 47–9
  food for thought 50–1
  foot off the gas improvisation 57
  improvised 57–9
  Ollie's Tip 49
  overthinking 50
  position-specific training 106–13
  right to play 53–4
  self-review 60–2
  young players 47–9
coaching staff 18–19
Coleman, Seamus 135–6, 181
commitment 158–9, 277–9
communication 52–5
compensation packages 208–9
competition 91–2
confidence 107
contacts 171
Conte, Antonio 198
contract negotiations 126–37
  Adam 131–7
  agents 126–30, 133–4, 135
  involvement 126–31
  Ollie's Tip 131
  Stewart 126–31
  walking away from 132
contracts 56, 208–9, 239, 241
control, lack of 5–6, 11–12
Cooper, Steve 89
cortisone levels 187
courage 60
Coventry City 42, 43
COVID-19 pandemic 210–15, 256
craftiness 23
Crewe Alexandra 16–17
crowd size 200–1
Crystal Palace 3, 11–12, 45, 120–1,
  216
  infrastructure 20–2
  parking the bus 100, 101
  press conferences 143–6
  shit incident 257–9
  staff 21
Cureton, Jamie 69, 131, 217–18, 221

Dalglish, Kenny 123, 282–3
Davis, Mabel, IH's debt to 243–5
decisions 1
defence coaching 47–9
defending 99–101
Delaney, Damien 144
delegating 112
Derby County 17, 246
determination 188
Di Matteo, Roberto 99
dieticians 21
dignity 283
disappointment 95
disillusionment 95
do, review and redo 222–3
dog trainers 94
Doherty, Tommy 43
dominating the ball 118–21
Downes, Wally 45
drag queens 185
drama 286–7
dress 260–5
Ducat, Gregory 171, 172–3, 174,
  177–9
Duffy, Jim 237
Dunford, Geoff 128, 129, 131
Durkin, Paul 151–2, 160–1
duty of care 150
Dyche, Sean 89

Eardley, Neil 181
Earnshaw, Rob 193
Ebanks-Blake, Sylvain 65, 68–70, 231
Edwards, Rob 164
Edwards, Shaun 113–14
effort, vs skill 277–9
Ellington, Nathan 69, 70–2, 182, 228
emotion 223, 286
empathy 156, 187–8
encouragement 2, 189
England 88
England women's team 87–8
enjoyment 2–3
enthusiasm 2, 102
European Championship 88
European Cup 43

Index

Euros, women's 87–8
Evans, Roy 283
Evatt, Ian 84, 164
Everson, Richard 181
Everton 18, 90, 141–2, 181
everyday life, food for thought 10
expectation levels 95
experience, importance 61
explaining 47–9

FA Cup 164–6, 179
failure 8, 60, 208–9
fairness 76–7, 155, 156, 166
fans 94, 95–8, 100, 103–4, 156, 158, 159
  dealing with 191–7
  intimidation 196
  Ollie's Tips 195, 197
  personal abuse 193–4
  and pundits 199–200
  suggestions 191–3
  and team selection 192
  thanking 194
Fashanu, Justin 184
fashion stakes 260–5
favouritism 93–5
Ferguson, Alex 94–5, 122–3, 145–6, 281, 281–2, 284, 286
Ferguson, Barry 156–7
Ferguson, Darren 281–2
Ferguson, Duncan 90
fighting 42–3
fighting your corner 205–8
fines 68, 85–6, 165–6
fireproof wellies 203
fitness, building 40
fitness coaches 114
Fleetwood Town 179–80
flexibility 27
focus 102
food for thought
  chairmen 180
  coaching 50–1
  inspiration 245
  managerial appointments 226
  managers 50–1

players 17, 28
principles of play 10
referees 152, 166–7
weakened teams 86
working with the media 147
football
  for anyone 87–8
  and life 285-7
Forbes, Terrell 81
Foster, Steve 218–22
fourth officials, point of 198–9
Francis, Gerry xii, 58, 73, 77, 112, 121, 124–5, 215–16, 234, 265, 278, 284–5
friendly matches 32, 259-60
friendships 114
Fulham 228
full-backs 119
Furlong, Paul 42–3, 107–10, 194–5

Gallen, Kevin 35–7, 38, 234, 273
gardening leave 225, 238–42, 275, 283
Gerrard, Steven 11
Giggs, Ryan 122
Gingal, John 114
Giroud, Oliver 180
Gould, Bobby 167
Gradi, Dario 16–17
Grant, Peter 237
Grimsby Town 29, 199, 210–15, 255–6
Guardiola, Pep 100, 124, 198, 264–5

habits 113
half-time team-talks 101
Hamburg 284
Harris, Neil 96
Harris, Vi 215, 216
Hasselbaink, Jimmy Floyd 266
Hayes 228
Hayles, Barry 69, 131, 182, 227, 228, 265
Heathlands School, St Albans 243–5
Heerenveen 63
Hibbitt, Kenny 216, 284–5

Index

Hodgson, Roy 286
Holloway, Bill xiv, 155, 190
Holloway, Ian
  Adam contract negotiations 131–7
  anger issue 4, 185–90
  Asda suit 264
  biggest strength 187–8
  bookings 152
  character default 4
  chequered past with match officials
    151, 152–68
  childhood 186
  daughters 202, 243–5, 260
  death of father 190
  disciplinary record 152–65
  early management career 50
  favourite signing 68–70
  fined 85–6
  first time as captain 167–8
  funniest signing 70–2
  gardening leave 225, 238–42, 275,
    283
  hang-up about hooter 7–8
  Ibiza Cup 42–4
  inspirations 280–7
  Iranian embassy dinner 268–71
  management career xiii
  marriage xiv
  matchday programme notes 202–4
  message 285–7
  at Millwall 45, 95–8
  Nigerian FA job offer 271–2
  personality 10
  playing career xii, 6
  pre-season ethos 46
  press conferences 143–8
  QPR transfer rumours 266–7
  RAF Aylesbury training 39–41
  RAF Kinloss training camp 33–9
  reputation 159–63, 168
  sense of humour 10
  son 185, 196
  squeamishness 270
  Stewart contract negotiations
    126–31
  Stress Test appearance 187–8
    strike rate 107
    style 99–100
    Sunderland sending off 164–6
    values 190
    vs Birmingham City 156–9
    worst signing 67–8
    see also individual clubs managed
Holloway, Jean xiv
Holloway, Kim xiv, 70–1, 148, 154–5,
    159, 161–2, 181–2, 186, 188,
    193, 194, 196, 212, 213, 218, 219,
    229, 242, 255, 264, 269, 282
homework 255–6
honesty 30, 60
Horner, Phil 18, 19
horses, team-talks to 250–2
Howard, Steven 181
Huddersfield Town 131
Hughton, Chris 89, 156–7, 158
Hull City 102

Ibiza, warm weather training 41–4
Ibiza Cup 42–4
Ibiza Town 42, 42–3
improvements, making 23–5
improvised training 57–9
Ince, Paul 137
Ince, Tom 137
individual, the 243–5
information, sharing 91–2
infrastructure 20–2
injured players 79
inspiration 243–5
intimidation 196
Inverness 38
Ipswich Town 225
Iranian embassy, dinner at 268–71

Jackett, Kenny 16
Jackson, Johnnie 90–1
Jedinak, Mile 144
job, hardest part 28
job offers, unusual 271–2
justice 155, 166

Kay, John 46

Index

Keane, Roy 164–6, 165, 222
Keegan, Kevin 127–8, 260, 283–4
Kite, Phil 218, 249–50
kitman 18, 19
Klopp, Jürgen 85–6, 100, 124, 198
knowledge 121

Lampard, Frank 18
Langley, Richard 147
lateness 222, 269
Latvia 205–6
leaders, good 9
leadership exercises 40
leadership style 1
League Cup 86
League Managers Association 209, 240, 282
learning environment 60
Leeds United 266–7
Leicester City 18, 22, 105, 179–80, 236–7
lending the ball 77–8
lessons
    from other sports 113–14
    from unlikely sources 185
life lessons 277–9
limitations 191–3
limits, pushing 41
Lincoln City 226
Liverpool 8, 11, 99, 123, 133–7, 281, 282–3, 284
loan players 169–70, 182–3
longevity 286
loopholes 209
losing, chance of 8
losing the dressing room 183–4

McCarthy, Mick 53, 85, 159–60, 168, 282
McDonald, Alan 278
McLaren, Steve 241, 267
management
    bottom line 53
    is about being in the shit xiii
managerial appointments 224–37
    agents 224

application process 224
and chemistry 228–36
club knowledge 226–8
feedback 225
food for thought 226
interviews 224–5, 229–30, 237
Ollie's Tip 235
presentations 226–8
managers, food for thought 50–1
Manchester City 8, 84, 99, 102, 141–2, 278, 286
Manchester United 69, 70, 84, 122–3, 145–6, 281, 286
Manning, Ryan 266
marking 124–5
Martinez, Roberto 117
Martyn, Nigel 215–16
match reports 139–40
matchday programme notes 202–4
matches, pre-season 32, 41–4
meals 25–8
media, working with 138–48
    food for thought 147
    handling questions 138–9, 143–4, 149
    match reports 139–40
    Ollie's Tip 141
    player protection 148–50
    press conferences 140–8
    quotes 142–3, 147, 147–8
media officer 18–19
Mellon, Micky 179–80
mental health 57–9, 189
    players 150
mental output, and physical output 57–8
mental training 40
Millwall 16, 45, 73, 95–8, 195–6
mindset 233
    centre-forwards 109, 111–12
    positive 6–9
moaners 78–9
money laundering 200–1
Montpellier 180
Moran, Ronnie 283
Moss, Jon 161–2

Index

motivation 6–9, 20, 102–5, 232–3
motivational speakers 103
Mourinho, Jose 99, 208, 284
Moyes, David 181
Moyes, Kenny 133–4, 135, 181
Muhammed Ali 280
Murray, Glenn 144, 146

naming and shaming 220
negative momentum 96
negativity 12
negotiating power 208–9
network building 14, 18
Newcastle United 127–8
Nigerian FA 271–2
nights out 38
Norris, David 231–5
Norwich City 8, 11, 73, 236–7
notebooks 101–2
Notts County 116
Nottingham Forest 89
numbers 93

Oatway, Charlie 258
Ollie's Tips
    agents 241
    anger management 185–90
    board members 235
    bollockings 223
    centre-forwards 110
    chairmen 177, 183
    coaching 49
    contract negotiations 131
    expect the unexpected 39
    fans 195, 197
    gardening leave 241
    habits 113
    managerial appointments 235
    media, working with 141
    personal touches 110
    player acquisitions 72, 177
    player protection 148–50
    players 15, 54
    post-match glass of wine 116–17
    pre-season 39, 44
    principles of play 4, 9

scouts 20
self-management 25
staff 20
starting XI selection 80–1
wives and girlfriends 15
orienteering 34–8
Ormerod, Brett 26–8, 246
other sports, lessons from 113–14
over-exuberance 45
owners 51, 205–8
Oyston, Karl 19, 24–5, 25–6, 85, 123, 132–3, 134–6, 166, 169–77, 177–9, 182–3, 205, 207

Paddy Power advert 250–2
Padula, Gino 81
Paladini, Gianni 44, 239–40, 267, 271–5
    shooting attempt 254–5
Palmer, Steve 234
Pardew, Alan 198
Paris Saint-Germain 51
Parish, Steve 21
parking the bus 99–101
passing lanes 120–1
passion 158–9
passports 67
pay-offs 208–9
Penrice, Gary 14–15, 16, 18, 63–4, 69, 70–1, 72, 106–12, 137, 169, 171–2, 180, 181, 182, 194–5, 206, 235
personal abuse, comeback 193–4
personal touches, Ollie's Tip 110
Peterborough 145–6, 281–2
PFA 241
Phillips, Kevin 146
physical output, and mental output 57–8
physios 18
Pilley, Andrew 179–80
player acquisitions 63–72
    agents 51–4
    COVID-19 pandemic 213–15
    creativity 72
    favourite signing 68–70

Index

funniest signing 70–2
missing out on 171–7, 181–2
Ollie's Tip 72, 177
sticking to principles 213–16
targets 206–7
unorthodox 63–7
worst signing 67–8
the wrong player 183–4
player protection 148–50
players
    assessing 15–18
    attitude 184
    chairman's 272–5
    character flaws 16
    dropped in 52–4
    duty of care 150
    fitness levels 248–50
    food for thought 17, 28
    getting the best out of 23
    improving 124–5
    injured 79
    keeping eye on 25–8
    letting go 28–9
    letting their hair down 38–9
    looking after 114
    mental health 150
    mindset 109, 111–12
    new 15–18
    non-selection 80–1
    Ollie's Tip 15, 54
    overthinking 50
    pushing 32
    relationship with 9–10
    right to play 53–4
    selling on 228
    vetting 67
    wives and girlfriends 15
    wrong 183–4
    young 20, 28, 47–9, 189
pleasing people 80
Plymouth Argyle 18, 159–63, 242
    David Norris episode 231–5
    Ebanks-Blake signing 68–70
    fans 194
    gym 23–4
    player acquisitions 63–7

relations with board 229–36
team plane 253–4
vs Real Madrid 259–60
police, relations with 33–4, 38, 64–7
policing, cost 73
Polter, Sebastian 266
Porto 284
Portugal 44
positive mindset 2, 6–9
post-match glass of wine 115–24
post-match press conferences 115,
    194
predictions 199–200
Premier League 21, 82–6, 99, 100,
    117–20, 123, 133, 146, 231
preparation 255–6
pre-season 31–46
    abroad 41–6
    character testing 31–2
    ethos 46
    expect the unexpected 39
    importance 31–2
    matches 32, 41–4
    nights out 38
    Ollie's Tip 39, 44
    role 31–2
    sessions 32
    training 32–42
    warm weather training 41–4
press conferences 115, 140–8, 194
Preston North End 19, 133
pride 212
principles, sticking to 213–16
principles of play 1–12
    encouragement 2
    enjoyment 2–3
    enthusiasm 2
    explaining 3
    following 9
    food for thought 10
    mapping 4
    Ollie's Tips 4, 9
    and outcomes 4–5
    in practice 3–12
    and tactics 10–11
problems 7

Index

provocation 196
Pulis, Tony 105, 121, 229, 231, 234,
    250
Puncheon, Jason 16, 134
pundits 199–200
Purnell, Phil 127–30

Queens Park Rangers 18, 67–8, 71, 73,
    103, 107–10, 154–5, 206, 228,
    229, 262–4, 268–71, 278–9, 285
    administration 28–9, 239–40
    budget 234
    chairman's player 272–5
    coaching 47–9
    fans 191–4, 194–5
    Francis as manager 58
    gardening leave 225, 238–42, 275,
        283
    Ibiza Cup 42–4
    player protection 148–50
    RAF Aylesbury training 39–41
    RAF Kinloss training camp 33–9
    relegated 234
    starting XI selection 77–9, 81
    transfer gossip 266–7
    use of motivator 6–9
    vote of confidence 254–5
    vs Cardiff 193–4
    vs Millwall 195–6
    vs Vauxhall Motors 191–3
    wage bill reduction 266
    Wimbledon merger talk 147–8
    wind-up merchants 275–7
Quinta do Lago 45
quotes 142–3, 147, 147–8

RAF 32
RAF Aylesbury 39–41
RAF Kinloss 33–9
Real Madrid 259–60
Redknapp, Harry 136
Reece, Andy 216
referees 151–68, 199
    buttering up 163
    convictions 168
    favourite 151–2
    food for thought 152, 166–7
    handling 163, 168
    IH and 151, 152–68
    notes 159–60
    personality 167–8
    preparation 159–61
    problem with 152
    questioning decisions 151–2
    reporting 153
    respect 163
    swearing 151
relaxation 245–7
resilience 188
resistance training 39–41
responsibility 155
rewards 46
Riga 205–6
Roberts, Jason 69, 108, 111–12, 182,
    228
Rodgers, Brendan 101
Roeder, Glenn 237
Romans 50
room service incident 25–8
Rooney, Wayne 122
Rose, Matty 81
Rotherham United 96–7
Rowlands, Martin 35–6
RuPaul's Drag Race 185

sacked in the morning 95–8
St Albans, Heathlands School 243–5
Sant Antoni de Portmany FC 42
Santos, Nuno Espírito 121–2
SAS training 31–2
Savage, Robbie 246
Scales, John 46
scientific element 24
scouts
    chief 14
    importance 20
    network 215
    Ollie's Tip 20
    retainer 20
    role 14

Index

Scunthorpe United 211, 284
second-hand clothes 262–4
Seip, Marcel 63–7
self-management 9–10, 25
self-review 60–2, 190
sending offs 155, 164–6
sexism 87
Shankly, Bill 63, 117
Sheepshanks, David 225
Sheffield Wednesday 103
shit (literal), dealing with 257–9
Shittu, Danny 171, 228, 272
signing-on fees 51
Sinclair, Scott 231
skill, vs effort 277–9
sleep on it 219
social media 87
Solskjaer, Ole Gunnar 94–5
Southampton 16
Southern, Keith 26–8, 117–18
Southgate, Gareth 88
Specsavers 166
splash and slide training 59
sport scientists 21
Sporting Chance 150
staff 13–22
    chief scout 14
    coaching 18–19
    importance 13–14
    infrastructure 20–2
    kitman 18, 19
    looking after 235, 237
    media officer 18–19
    network building 14, 18
    Ollie's Tip 20
    physio 18
    scouts 20
    and success 14
    terms 235
starting XI selection 76–81
    advice 79–80
    going with your gut 79–80
    mantra 80–1
    naming 76
    non-selection 80–1
    Ollie's Tip 80–1

own way of doing 80
    physical process 79
Stevenage 228
Stewart, Marcus 126–31
Stoke 73, 231, 234
stress relief 58–9
Stress Test 187–8
success, and staff 14
suits 260–1, 264
Sunderland 164–6, 194, 222, 253–4
superstition 92–3, 265
support, lack of 203
sweeteners 200–2
Sylvestre, Ludovic 84

tactics 10–11, 50
Taylor, Graham 79–80, 219–20
Taylor-Fletcher, Gary 117
team, weakened
    fielding 82–6
    food for thought 86
team ownership 52–4
team sports, managing 60–1
team-talks 101, 102–5, 245–7
    to horses 250–2
teamwork missions 40
technical areas 198–9
Thompson, Andy 218–22
Thompson, Steve 18, 19, 59
Three Es, the 1–12
    encouragement 2
    enjoyment 2–3
    enthusiasm 2
    explaining 3
    following 9
    food for thought 10
    mapping 4
    Ollie's Tips 4, 9
    and outcomes 4
    in practice 3–12
    and tactics 10–11
thugs 96–8
Torres, Fernando 99
Tottenham Hotspur 83, 85–6, 136
touchline attire 264–5
touchline banter 276–7

Index

tracksuits 260–1
training
    abroad 41–6
    ballet 59
    dress 261
    foot off the gas 57
    improvised 57–9
    leadership exercises 40
    mental 40
    orienteering 34–8
    position-specific 106–13
    pre-season 32–42
    resistance 39–41
    runs 220–2
    splash and slide 59
    teamwork missions 40
    warm weather 41–4
training camps 32–9
training grounds 24–5
Tranmere Rovers 255–6
transfer gossip 265–8
transfer war chests 205–8
travelling 253–4
triallists 213–16
trust 56, 74, 230
truth 30, 78–9
Turkey 177–9
25-man squad lists 82–6
Twitter 196

Udinese 172–173, 174, 176
unexpected, expect the 39

values 190
Vardy, Jamie 179–80
Varney, Luke 16–17
Vaughan, David 134, 246
Vauxhall Motors 191–3

Walcott, Theo 117
Wales, Steve 18, 19
Walton & Hersham 70–1
Ward, John 265
wardrobe 260–5
warm weather training 41–4
Warnock, Neil 154, 162–3, 275–7,
    282, 286
Wasps Rugby Club 113–14
Watford 228
weakened teams
    fielding 82–6
    food for thought 86
Wegerle, Roy 278–9
Wenger, Arsène 86, 118–21, 198, 281
Wiegman, Sarina 88
Wigan 117, 228
Wilkins, Ray 77–8, 223, 262–4, 285
Williams, Matt 18–19, 19, 132–3, 134,
    135, 158, 162, 207
Williams, Tommy 81
Wilson, Clive 264
Wimbledon xii, 30, 45, 46, 80
winning 8
Wise, Dennis 30
wives and girlfriends, Ollie's Tip 15
Wolverhampton Wanderers 121–2,
    159–60
Women's football 87–8
World Cup 88
Wyscout.com 180

"Yeah, I'm all of that plus a bag of
    chips" comeback 193–4

Zaha, Wilfried 143–6, 258–9
Zamora, Bobby 131
Zigic, Nikola 156–7